Modeling and Animation Using Blender

Blender 2.80: The Rise of Eevee

Ezra Thess Mendoza Guevarra

Apress®

Modeling and Animation Using Blender: Blender 2.80: The Rise of Eevee

Ezra Thess Mendoza Guevarra
Laguna, Philippines

ISBN-13 (pbk): 978-1-4842-5339-7   ISBN-13 (electronic): 978-1-4842-5340-3
https://doi.org/10.1007/978-1-4842-5340-3

Managing Director, Apress Media LLC: Welmoed Spahr
Acquisitions Editor: Spandana Chatterjee
Development Editor: Matthew Moodie
Coordinating Editor: Shrikant Vishwakarma

Cover designed by eStudioCalamar

Cover image designed by Tiago Pereira Lourenço from Blender Artist community

Distributed to the book trade worldwide by Springer Science+Business Media New York, 233 Spring Street, 6th Floor, New York, NY 10013. Phone 1-800-SPRINGER, fax (201) 348-4505, e-mail orders-ny@springer-sbm.com, or visit www.springeronline.com. Apress Media, LLC is a California LLC and the sole member (owner) is Springer Science + Business Media Finance Inc (SSBM Finance Inc). SSBM Finance Inc is a **Delaware** corporation.

For information on translations, please e-mail rights@apress.com, or visit http://www.apress.com/rights-permissions.

Apress titles may be purchased in bulk for academic, corporate, or promotional use. eBook versions and licenses are also available for most titles. For more information, reference our Print and eBook Bulk Sales web page at http://www.apress.com/bulk-sales.

Any source code or other supplementary material referenced by the author in this book is available to readers on GitHub via the book's product page, located at www.apress.com/978-1-4842-5339-7. For more detailed information, please visit http://www.apress.com/source-code.

Printed on acid-free paper

To Father God
To my mother and father
To my friends and fellow Filipinos
To all PWDs

Table of Contents

TABLE OF CONTENTS

TABLE OF CONTENTS

About the Author

Ezra Thess Mendoza Guevarra graduated with a Bachelor of Science in information technology from STI College in the Philippines. Though she graduated with web developer/designer knowledge, her passion for the arts that started in childhood never went away. In 2016, she became interested in 3D modeling and tried to create a game with a team.

She also loves research. She created ezrathessguevarra4.wixite.com/yorozuyaezra to share the knowledge she gained through her research and share her creativity. She has also served as a government employee in the Philippines.

Despite being epileptic, she continues to pursue her dreams and "break the walls." A researcher and a passionate artist, Ezra is currently using her skills as a freelancer.

About the Technical Reviewer

Mieren Taylor is a 3D generalist who works with independents and small businesses to create product visuals and promotional material, as well as patch pipelines in various productions. Some of the projects she's worked on include making 3D sarees for Yes!Poho, creating 3D visuals for Kairma air filters, and logo design for Tjoobloom. She has worked with Blender as a freelancer for more than five years and has every intention to carry on using this amazing software and exploring the new features of its latest version.

You can see Mieren's latest work on her website at www.Tomations.com.

Acknowledgments

There are a lot of people I'd like to thank. This book was produced by me alone.

First and foremost, I'd like to thank Father God for giving me this opportunity, and also for giving me the knowledge and skills I needed throughout the process. He's my number-one partner here.

I'd like to thank Mrs. Cecilia Guevarra, my mother, and Mr. Alexander Guevarra, my father, for their patience and support in many aspects.

I'd like to thank the HIJCC family for your prayers and support.

I'd like to thank the Apress staff, who gave their time and effort on this book, especially Ms. Spandana Chatterjee, Mr. Shrikant Vishwakarma, Mr. Matthew Moodie, and Ms. Mieren Taylor.

I'd also like to thank my friends. I will not mention any names but you know who you are. You support me in many aspects of my life.

I'd like to thank my previous employers, especially the PNR family and the GAP family for every memories and experiences.

Lastly, I'd like to thank you, my dear reader.

Introduction

Good morning! Good afternoon! Good evening! Wherever you are reading this book, I'd like first to greet you, my dear reader. Welcome to the world of 3D and welcome to the world of Blenderers.

I first searched, "What is the best 3D software for beginners?" in Google. You might already know that Blender 3D is "free." In this book, I discuss what "free" means, and what the Blender license means.

When I started learning 3D, I only played with the 3D viewer and Paint3D applications that are in Windows 10. But those applications have limitations. I decided to research 3D software that could meet my needs on a laptop. You might think, obviously a PC is better than a laptop. Originally, I'm a web developer/designer, and because 3D has become a part of web design, I decided to study 3D concepts.

Blender 3D met my needs. It launches fast, even on my laptop. I can design the model that I want. There's a lot of community and tutorials out there and it's free.

This book is a tour of Blender 2.80, in which its newest render engine is rendered in real time; it's called Eevee. They called this latest version a "game-changer" because it has a lot of changes—from the user interface to its tools, which is especially helpful to beginners and laptop users like me.

Since I called it a tour, Chapter 1 shows you the basics, like installation and features. In Chapter 2, I discuss modeling tools. In Chapter 3, I discuss the tools used in animation. In Chapter 4, I discuss things related to the game engine.

I also discuss Blender 2.80 hotkeys and refraction, which is helpful for those who are interested in photorealism.

I suggest that you install Blender 2.80 before Chapter 2. I want you experiment with every tool I mention so that you know which tools will be useful for you in the future.

So, let's end the introduction here and proceed to our tour! Enjoy learning!

CHAPTER 1

The Tour

Blender is a 3D content creation suite that offers a broad range of essential tools, including modeling, rendering, animation, video editing, VFX, compositing, texturing, rigging, and many simulation types. It is cross-platform with an OpenGL GUI that is uniform across all major platforms. It can customize with Python scripts. If you have heard of or tried 3DS Max, Maya, Cinema4D, SketchUp, Wings3D, or Adobe Dimension, and if you've used Windows 10, 3D Viewer, and ArtistGL, then you have a basic idea of what Blender 3D is.

Why Blender?

There are a lot of 3D software packages around the globe. There's 3Ds Max, Maya, Cinema4D, Wings3D, Modo, Daz3D, SketchUp, and a lot more. I have personal reasons for preferring Blender over the others, but I gathered reviews from across the Internet.

Hidden Tools

There are a lot of built-in add-ons in Blender that you can explore to make your project a lot easier. Add-ons need to be activated. There are also free add-ons that you can download that are made by developers in the community.

Blender has a lot to offer its users. There are a lot of tools to learn that you will enjoy. You will discover a lot of things that you will find helpful, such as shaders. Creating outstanding materials or shaders in Blender can't be discussed in one go. There are a lot of things involved, but learning the style and techniques can help you make something like Pixar shades.

© Ezra Thess Mendoza Guevarra 2020
E. T. M. Guevarra, *Modeling and Animation Using Blender*, https://doi.org/10.1007/978-1-4842-5340-3_1

Launches Quickly

Personally, speed is what brings me to Blender. A lot of software takes time to launch, especially if another application is running. But with Blender, this isn't a problem. It only takes seconds to launch and start your project.

Customizable Interface

The ability to customize the Blender interface based on your preferences is one of the features that attracts many of its users.

Significant Upgrades

If you read the Blender version milestones, you will notice how the team upgrades Blender. In every version, there are major upgrades, fixes, and new developments by its developers. That makes you always look forward to the new version.

Workflow Speed

At first, as with other software, you are slow in making your project; but after you learn all the shortcut keys in Blender, you will notice how quickly you are making your project. The fact that everything in Blender has a shortcut key makes sense. You don't need to memorize it all. Most of the artists in the Blender community use a cheat sheet for the Blender hotkeys. I provide it in this book.

Blender Cycles Built-in Renderer

Blender offers an unbiased, physically based, pathtracing engine that simulates the way a camera works in the real world. It is optimized for GPU animation and rendering.

The Community

There's a large community that supports Blender. A lot of volunteers, both developers and artists, are there to assist Blender users around the globe. You not only gain support as a user, you also gain connections and friends, which are more important.

The following is a list of Blender communities from Blender.org.

- `https://blender.stackexchange.com`: Question-and-answer site for people who use Blender to create 3D graphics, animations, or games.

- `https://blenderartists.org`: One of the most active independent user sites.

- `https://blender.community/c/today`: User-submitted stories, chat, and weekly live streams.

- `www.blendernation.com`: An overview of everything Blender—development updates, new tutorials, artwork, and community information.

- `https://blender.chat/home`: Independent chat server created to help Blender users to communicate in real time. Part of the blender. community network.

- `https://discordapp.com/invite/blender`: Community-managed discord server.

- `https://blender.community/c/rightclickselect/`: Ideas for Blender.

- `https://blender.community/c/graphicall/`: Custom Blender builds by users and developers from the community.

- `www.reddit.com/r/blender/`: A very active subreddit devoted to Blender; news, critics, and a monthly contest.

- `www.facebook.com/groups/BNPRandFreestyle/`: Facebook group for sharing Blender-based non-photorealistic rendering (NPR) techniques and styles.

- `www.blendswap.com`: A community of passionate Blender artists who share their work under Creative Common licenses.

- `http://bbug.be/`

- `www.facebook.com/groups/2207257375`

- `www.blendercn.org`: A Chinese Blender community.

- `www.bgteach.com`: A Chinese Blender community.

- `dbc-3d.nl/`: A Dutch Blender community.

- `https://blender.community/c/actu/`: A French Blender community.

- `http://blenderlounge.fr/`: A French Blender community.

- `http://blenderclan.tuxfamily.org/html/modules/news/`: A French Blender community.

- `www.nurembug.org`: A German Blender community.

- `www.meetup.com/Blender-3D-Meetup-Munchen/`: A German Blender community.

- `https://blendpolis.de/`: A German Blender Community.

- `www.facebook.com/groups/BlenderGreece/`: A Greek Blender community.

- `http://forum.blender.org.il/`: A Hebrew Blender community.

- `https://blender.community/c/oggi/`: An Italian Blender community.

- `www.blender.it/`; An Italian Blender community.

- `https://blender.jp/`: A Japanese Blender Community.

- `www.facebook.com/groups/blender3d.msia`: A Malaysian Blender community.

- `https://polskikursblendera.pl/`: A Polish Blender community.

- `www.facebook.com/groups/blenderpolska/`: A Polish Blender community.

- `www.blender.pl/index.php?action=portal`: A Polish Blender community.

- `https://blender.community/c/hoje/`: A Portuguese Blender community.

- `http://forum.blender-pt.com/`: A Portuguese Blender community.

- `https://vk.com/blender_3d`: A Russian Blender community.

- `http://blender3d.org.ua/`: A Russian Blender community.

- `https://blender.community/c/hoy/`: A Spanish Blender community.

- `www.facebook.com/groups/HubLa/`: A Spanish Blender community.

- `www.facebook.com/groups/blenderpo/`: A Spanish Blender community.

- `www.facebook.com/groups/blendeame/`: A Spanish Blender community.

- `https://discordapp.com/invite/ebpM5nE`: A Spanish Blender community.

Open Source Software

Aside from being "free," open source software gives you the right to modify your copy and make a version that suits your needs. This is important, mostly for large companies, because not everything you want can be available in one software program. Usually, you need two or three software licenses to create an outstanding CGI film, but sometimes, that's hard. If your company has an IT department, and you know that they can build add-ons that provide features similar to what you want in licensed software, then you need open source software to freely insert these features. Since open source software can be freely modified, you will not have a problem configuring its code.

Note There is free software, open source software, and freeware. Their differences are in licensing. Since Blender is GNU GPL, it is considered both free software and open source software. Being free doesn't mean the price; it means freedom. It's the freedom to choose the way you distribute, the freedom to change the program, the freedom to redistribute copies, and the freedom to distribute your modified version of the program under the GNU GPL license.

Blender's Future Is Bright

Blender's future is bright because of the upgrade the team did for Blender 2.80, or what they call Eevee. They added a new built-in renderer, and changed the layout of its interface, which makes it user-friendly and easy for both beginners and advanced users of Blender.

Blender 2.80 is a version to look forward to, and that's the topic that I discuss next.

What's with Blender 2.80?

What should we look forward to in Blender version 2.80? There's a lot, but the following are the top five reasons.

User Interface

Blender 2.80 has a revamped user interface. Tools, gizmos, and consistent layouts make it easier to discover and use Blender's many features.

Workspaces let you quickly get started with tasks like sculpting, texture painting, or motion tracking. They can be customized to create your own work environment.

Figure 1-1 shows the Blender 2.80 user interface.

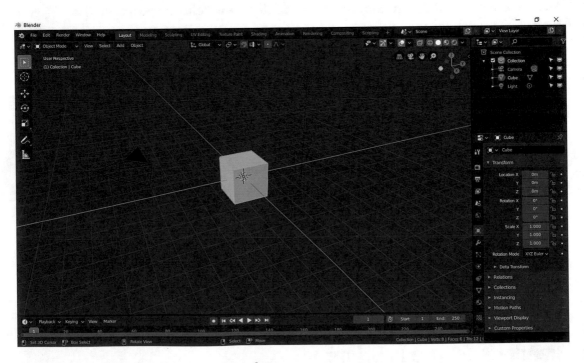

Figure 1-1. *Blender 2.80 user interface*

In Figure 1-1, you see the menus for layout, modeling, sculpting, UV editing, texture painting, shading, animation, rendering, compositing, and scripting. These menus let you quickly switch to the workspace you want for your project. Each workspace can be customized according to your own preferences.

Eevee

Eevee is a new physically based real-time renderer. It works as a renderer for final frames and as the engine driving Blender's real-time viewport for creating assets.

It has advanced features, such as volumetrics, screen-space reflections and refractions, subsurface scattering, soft, and contact shadows, depth of field, and camera motion blur and bloom.

Viewport

There is a new, modern 3D viewport. The workbench engine can visualize your scene in flexible ways. Eevee powers the viewport for interactive modeling and painting with PBR materials.

If you're wondering about the viewport, it allows you to see your objects and manipulate them. This area is called the viewport.

The minimum graphics card requirement for Blender has increased to OpenGL 3.3.

2D Animation

Blender's 2D drawing capabilities have greatly improved in 2.80. The new Grease Pencil focus creates a friendlier interface for the 2D artist, while keeping the advantages of a full 3D suite.

Grease Pencil is no longer just a stroke; it's now a real Blender object with huge improvements to brushes and tools.

Cycles

Cycles is a renderer that has been built into Blender since version 2.61. It is very efficient at rendering photorealistic images.

There are new principled volume shaders, hair shaders, and bevel and ambient occlusion shaders. The industry-standard Cryptomatte is now fully supported, combining your CPU and GPU for rendering, random-walk subsurface scattering and many other improvements.

Note   Random Walk Subsurface Scattering is a shader for subsurface scattering mode, which is used in texturing skins. Subsurface scattering is when light passes an object, which is normally opaque, like our skin and plastics.

Figure 1-2 is an example of a scene made in 2.80 and rendered in Cycles.

Figure 1-2.   *Witch by Mohamad from blenderartist.org*

Installation

System Requirements

If you are using Blender to create 3D models and assets only, the minimum requirements will do. But if you will use Blender for bigger projects, you need to invest in hardware.

Figure 1-3 shows Blender's system requirements.

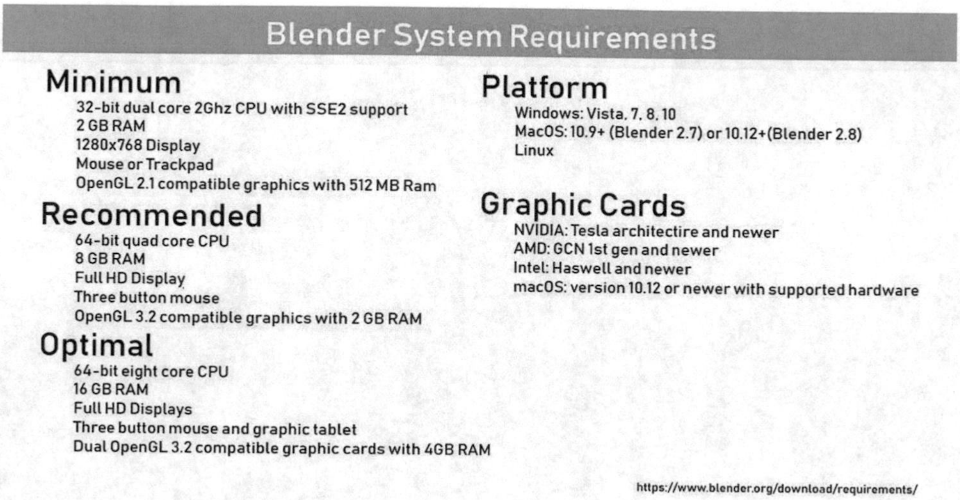

Blender System Requirements

Minimum
32-bit dual core 2Ghz CPU with SSE2 support
2 GB RAM
1280x768 Display
Mouse or Trackpad
OpenGL 2.1 compatible graphics with 512 MB Ram

Recommended
64-bit quad core CPU
8 GB RAM
Full HD Display
Three button mouse
OpenGL 3.2 compatible graphics with 2 GB RAM

Optimal
64-bit eight core CPU
16 GB RAM
Full HD Displays
Three button mouse and graphic tablet
Dual OpenGL 3.2 compatible graphic cards with 4GB RAM

Platform
Windows: Vista, 7, 8, 10
MacOS: 10.9+ (Blender 2.7) or 10.12+(Blender 2.8)
Linux

Graphic Cards
NVIDIA: Tesla architectire and newer
AMD: GCN 1st gen and newer
Intel: Haswell and newer
macOS: version 10.12 or newer with supported hardware

https://www.blender.org/download/requirements/

Figure 1-3. *Blender system requirements*

Installation Process

There are two ways to install Blender: using the .exe file or using the .zip file.

Figure 1-4 shows you where to download.

At www.blender.org, click the Download Blender 2.80 button to automatically download the .exe file of Blender's current release.

If you go to www.blender.org/download, you see all the links to install current and past versions.

Note   The difference between the .exe installer and the .zip installer is that when you use .exe installer, all of its components—the registry and every detail regarding the software—are installed on your PC or laptop. The software creates a directory in the C drive, with backup files, so if ever you accidentally uninstall the program, and install it again, whatever you did before (e.g., any configuration) is remembered by the software. With a .zip file, that doesn't apply. After you extract the .zip file, the program is there. Portable software. It can be transferred to a flash drive and run on any PC. Save the file on the flash drive too. You can choose either according to your preference.

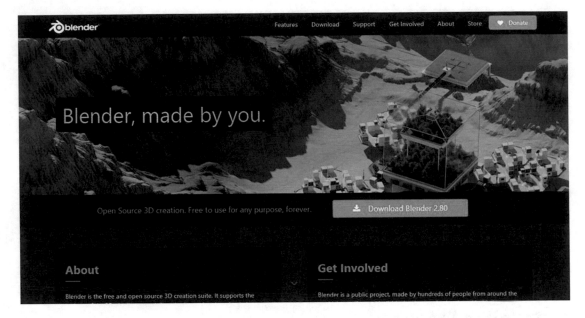

Figure 1-4. *Download from Blender.org*

Figure 1-5 shows you one of the keynotes when installing, not only Blender, but in general.

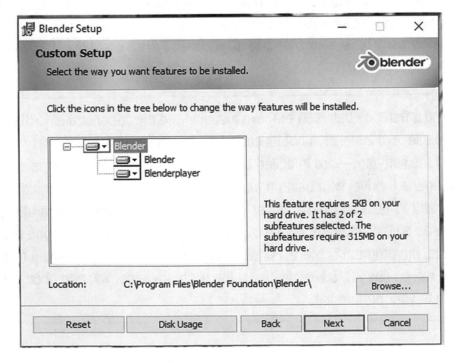

Figure 1-5. *Installation with .exe*

Note   It is always recommended to install software in C:\Program Files, but you also have the option to install it on the D: drive to free your C: drive. Click the Browse button. Make sure to create a folder of the software on the D: drive before installing it there. Another thing to note is if you have a previous version of Blender on your machine, you are offered the chance to change, repair, or remove Blender at the start of installation. The correct choice is to Change it.

Blender gives you an option to use either the .exe file or the .zip file. You can download and use WinRAR to extract the .zip file or to use the default zip extractor on Windows.

Figures 1-6, 1-7, and 1-8 show the process of extracting Blender using the .zip file.

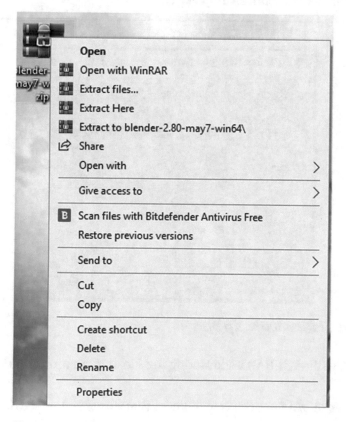

Figure 1-6. *Installation with .zip part 1*

In Figure 1-6, you can choose **Extract Here**, **Extract files...**, or **Extract to <folder name>**. When you choose Extract here, whatever files are inside it are extracted in the place where it is. For example, in Figure 1-7, all the Blender files are extracted to the desktop. It is extracted the way it was compressed as a zip. What this mean is that if the files were not in a folder, they are extracted unorganized in the place you extracted them to. Extract Files gives you the option to choose where you will extract the files, and there are other options in Settings that might help. **Extract to <folder name>** makes the program create a folder before it extracts the files inside. This tip is applicable, not only in Blender but also in other software. I always choose **Extract to <folder name>** since it is organized and fast.

Note   In vanilla Windows 10, the same function is achieved with the only extract option in the right-click menu: Extract All....

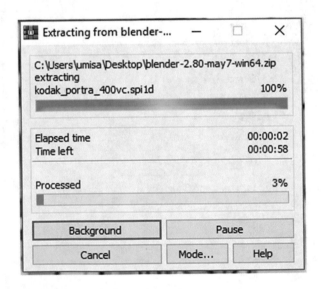

Figure 1-7. Installation with .zip part 2

In Figure 1-7, while WinRAR is extracting the file, it is creating a folder on my desktop.

When it comes to .zip files, the way to know that this was done is after the window that processes the extraction is closed, you see that your folder already has all of its contents.

Let's run Blender 2.80 and take a look at its user interface.

The Face of Blender 2.80

Let's discuss the new look of Blender's user interface.

Blender's user interface is designed to be non-overlapping, which means that you can view all relevant options and tools at a glance without pushing and dragging editors around. It is also designed to be non-blocking. Tools and interface options do not block the users from any other parts of Blender. It is designed with non-modal tools, which means that the tools can be accessed efficiently without taking time to select between other tools.

As you can see in Figure 1-8, Blender's interface is separated into three areas.

- The Topbar is at the top

- The editor is in the middle area

- The Status Bar is at the bottom

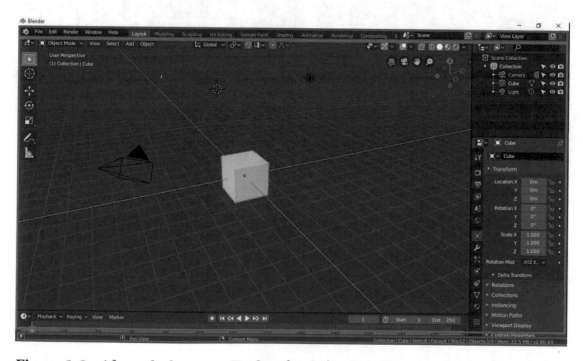

Figure 1-8. *After splash screen: Topbar (violet), editor area (green), Status Bar(blue)*

The Blender default startup shows the Layout workspace in the editor screen. The following is what you see in this workspace.

- 3D view in the top left

- Timeline in the bottom left

- Outliner in the top right

- Properties in the bottom right

Figure 1-9 shows the components of an editor.

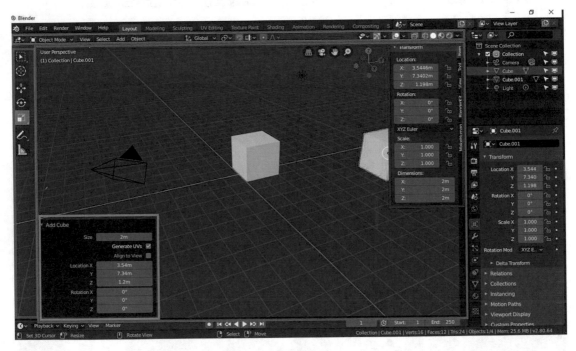

Figure 1-9. *3D view editor: the header (yellow), main region (green), toolbar (violet), sidebar (red), and operator panel (blue)*

In general, an editor is used to view and modify your work. Editors are divided into regions, and regions can have smaller elements called *panels* and *tabs*.

- The header in the 3D view editor is mainly used to switch the editing mode—from object mode to edit mode or to sculpting mode. I discuss these modes in Chapter 2. In this header, you can also add meshes by clicking Add ➤ Mesh ➤ the object you want to add. An easier way to do this is to hold Shift and press A.

- The main region is where you see all the editing you've done.

- The toolbar guides you with basic functions, like moving an object, measuring the object's size, scaling, rotating, and making annotations.

- The sidebar is where you see the exact measurements, such as the current location of the object, the scale size, the rotation value, and dimensions.

Customization

Another great thing about Blender is that it allows you to customize everything—including the themes and the shortcut keys for your own convenience.

To customize your themes or shortcut keys, go to Edit ➤ Preferences. Figure 1-10 shows the Blender Preferences window.

Figure 1-10. *User preferences*

Blender opens a new window in which you can edit your preferences. You have the option to minimize the window.

You can change the resolution scale if you want everything to be larger than the usual; set this in Interface ➤ Resolution Scale. You can change the colors of each workspace in the Themes menu, as shown in Figure 1-11.

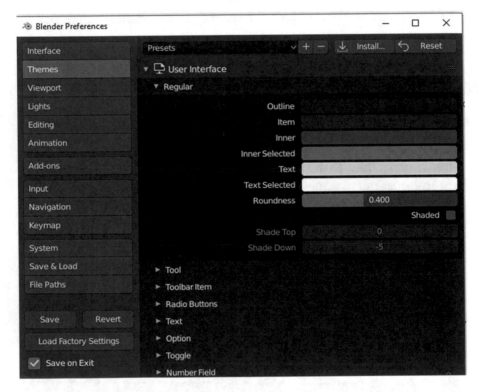

Figure 1-11. *User preference: Themes*

You can add or explore more add-ons in the Add-ons menu, as shown in Figure 1-12.

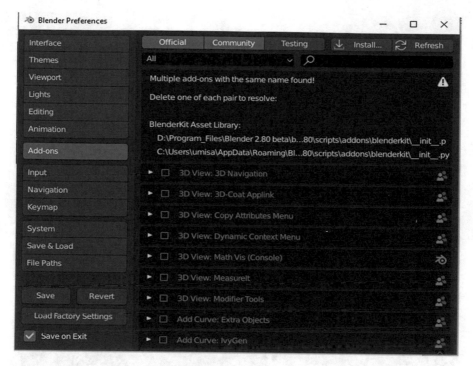

Figure 1-12. *User preference: Add-ons*

Blender is known for making project workflows faster through its shortcuts. You can change shortcuts in the Keymap menu, as shown in Figure 1-13.

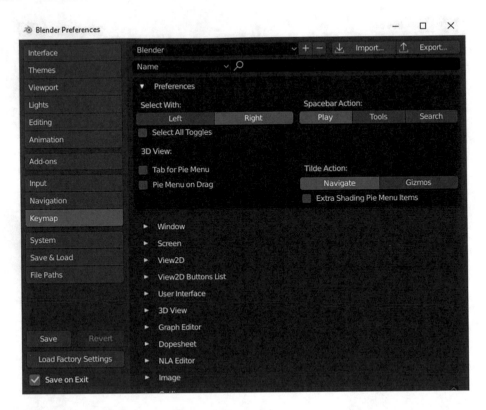

Figure 1-13. *User preference: Keymap*

If you are using a laptop or a PC with a two-button mouse, you can go to the Input menu and check the Emulate Numpad option in the Keyboard panel to enable the shortcut keys to involve the numpad keys. Check the Emulate 3 Button Mouse option in the Mouse panel to enable the shortcut that substitutes your mouse key, as shown in Figure 1-14.

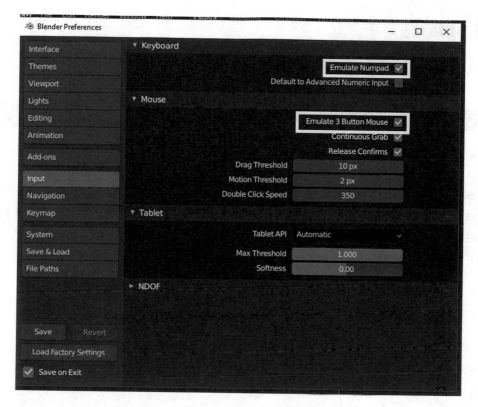

Figure 1-14. User preference: Input

When you activate Emulate 3 Button Mouse, you can use Alt+Left mouse button and drag to rotate the view. Use Shift+Alt+left mouse button and drag to pan the view. You can change the Selection button in the mouse from left mouse to right mouse in Keymap section, under Preferences ➤ Select with.

If you're using a Mac with a single-button mouse, Option+mouse button is the equivalent of a middle button mouse. To rotate the view, press Option+mouse button and drag. To pan the view, press Shift+Option+mouse button and drag. To select an object, press the Command button+mouse button. You can create loop cuts without a scroll wheel by using the PageUp/PageDown or Up/Down keys, or by entering a numeric key after pressing Ctrl+R.

Workspaces

Figure 1-15 shows the default workspaces in Blender.

Figure 1-15. *Workspaces*

Blender has ten workspaces to play around in. Workspaces are essentially predefined window layouts. You can create your own customized workspaces by clicking the plus icon beside the Scripting tab.

The following are Blender's predefined workspaces.

- Layout: The general workspace to preview and work on your project.

- Modeling: The workspace for modifying geometry with modeling tools.

- Sculpting: The workspace for modifying geometry with sculpting tools.

- UV Editing: The workspace for mapping image textures in 3D objects.

- Texture Painting: The workspace for coloring image textures in 3D.

- Shading: The workspace for applying color/nodes and shades in 3D.

- Animation: The workspace for applying animation effects.

- Rendering: The workspace for rendering the final image.

- Compositing: The workspace for post processing.

- Scripting: The workspace for editing and adding Python script or code.

Note   Workspaces are automatically saved in a .blend file. When opening the file, if you check the Loud-UI option in the Blender file browser, Blender will override the current layout and use the layout saved in the .blend file.

Figure 1-16 shows the layout workspace, which by default is the first thing that you see after the Blender flash screen.

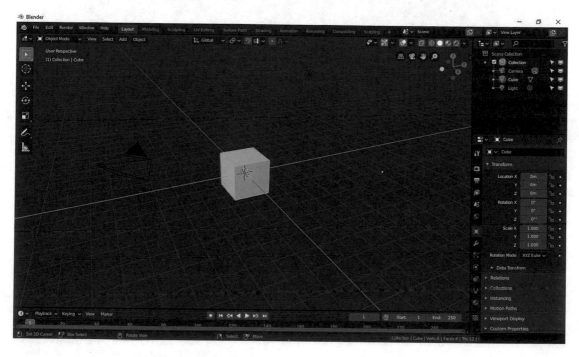

Figure 1-16. *Workspaces: Layout*

Areas

Figure 1-17 shows a part of an area.

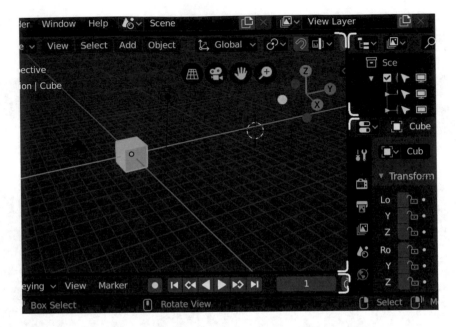

Figure 1-17. *Areas*

The application window is divided into a number of areas that reserve screen space for editors, such as 3D view, outliner, timeline, properties, and more. The boundaries of an area are indicated by rounded corners, as shown in Figure 1-17.

By dragging a rounded corner, which is highlighted in yellow, you can duplicate the existing editor. For example, if you drag the rounded corner of a 3D view editor, it opens another 3D view editor.

You can resize areas by dragging with the left mouse button. Move your mouse cursor over the border between two areas, so that the cursor changes to a double-headed arrow, and then click and drag.

Splitting an area creates a new area. Joining two areas closes one area. To do this, place the mouse cursor in an area corner; the cursor will change to a cross or plus sign. Press the left mouse button to activate a splitting or a joining command. Dragging the area inward makes the areas split, whereas dragging the area outward makes two areas in a similar size and the editors join.

Toggle Maximize Window/Fullscreen

To maximize the area, go to View ➤ Area ➤ Toggle Maximize Area or press Ctrl+spacebar. To return to normal size, you can use the Ctrl+spacebar shortcut or click the Back to Previous button on the Topbar.

Figure 1-18 shows the maximized screen.

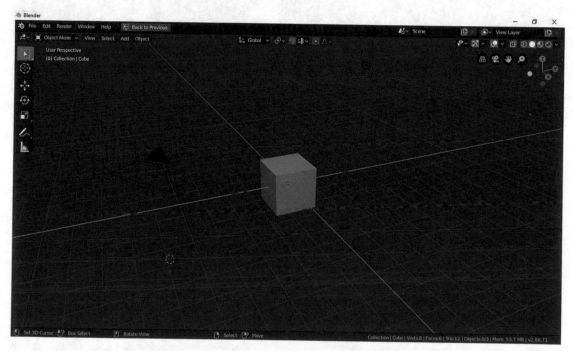

Figure 1-18. *Maximize screen*

To use the fullscreen mode, go to View ➤ Area ➤ Toggle Fullscreen Area or press Ctrl+Alt+spacebar. To return to normal size, use the keyboard shortcut.

Fullscreen mode is shown in Figure 1-19.

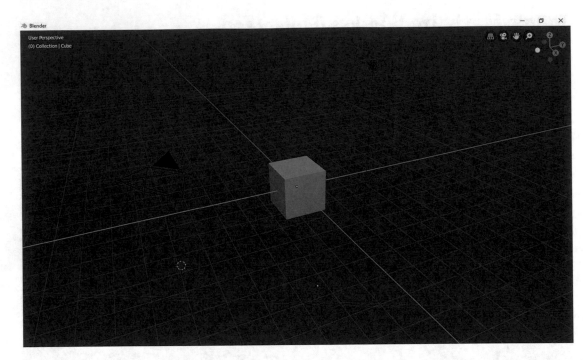

Figure 1-19. *Fullscreen*

Editors

Figure 1-20 shows the list of editors.

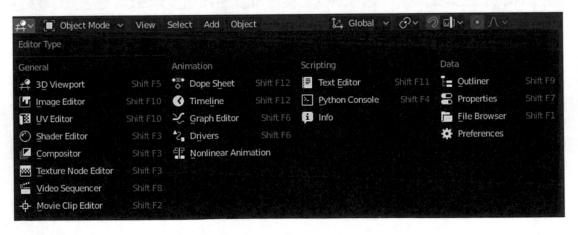

Figure 1-20. *Editors*

Blender provides editors for displaying and modifying different aspects of data. The Editor Type selector (the first button on the left side of a header) allows you to change the editor in that area. This helps you to create an ideal workspace for your project. Every area may contain any type of editor; it is also possible to open the same type multiple times.

I'll discuss the tools that are used for modeling in the next chapter. Let's end this first chapter with a sample render from Cheryl Chen, as shown in Figure 1-21.

Figure 1-21. *In The Wind by Cheryl Chen*

Blending with Blender: Getting Started

Here we are at Chapter 2 of our book. You'll be expected to learn a lot: the basic tools for modeling in Blender 2.80, including the Layout workspace, and the tools for lighting. The chapter starts with a tour of the tools before it finishes with a sample project that uses these tools.

I'll be discussing a lot, so let's end the introduction and get started.

Modeling with Blender 2.80

The creation of a 3D scene needs four components: the model, the materials, the lights, and the camera. First, I'll talk about modeling. Modeling is the art of making three-dimensional models. *Three-dimensional* means that there is length (pertaining to the y axis), breadth (pertaining to the x axis), and depth (pertaining to the z axis).

In Figure 2-1, you see a sample emphasizing the basic parts of a 3D model.

© Ezra Thess Mendoza Guevarra 2020
E. T. M. Guevarra, *Modeling and Animation Using Blender*, https://doi.org/10.1007/978-1-4842-5340-3_2

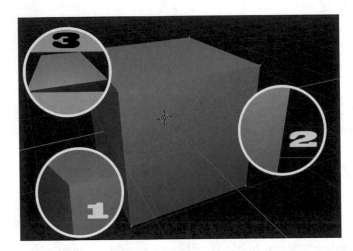

Figure 2-1. *Basic 3D model (Ellipse 1: Vertices, Ellipse 2: Edges, Ellipse 3: Faces)*

In Figure 2-1, you see the three basic parts of a 3D model being emphasized in the ellipses: the vertices, the edge, and the face. The vertex is a small dot that when connected, forms an edge. Edges are line segments that, when connected, form the face. Faces are the planes that, when connected, form an object.

Let's look at Figure 2-2.

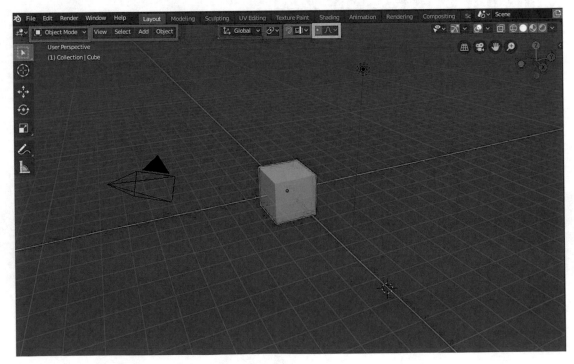

Figure 2-2. *Layout workspace*

Let's discuss what's in Figure 2-2. Inside the yellow box is **Edit mode**, which is set to **Object mode** in the figure. Blender has six kinds of modes, but the number of active modes depends on the type of objects you are using or modifying. So before we get to the menus, we should cover the basics of objects.

Types of Objects

Mesh

Mesh is active in Object mode, Edit mode, Sculpt mode, Vertex Paint, Weight Paint, and Texture Paint. Mesh is a commonly used object in creating scenes.

Figure 2-3 shows examples of meshes.

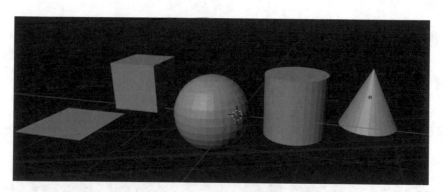

Figure 2-3. *Example meshes*

Curve and Surface

Curve and Surface are active in Object mode and Edit mode. Both are expressed in mathematical functions, and if you know Illustrator and Photoshop well, it works is the same as paths. They are defined by control points.

Figure 2-4 shows Curve and Surface examples.

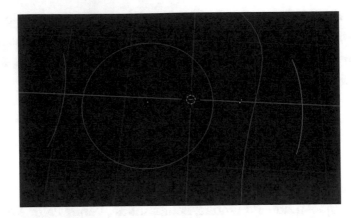

Figure 2-4. *Example of Curves and Surfaces*

Metaball

Metaball is active in Object mode and Edit mode. Metaballs are not defined by vertices (unlike meshes), and they are not defined by control points (unlike curves and surfaces). Meta objects are literally mathematical formulas that are calculated on the fly by Blender.

Figure 2-5 shows examples of metaballs.

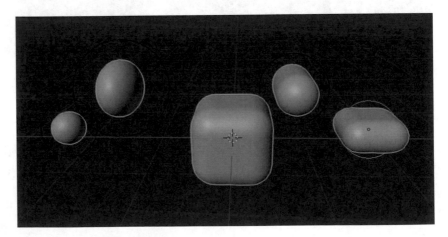

Figure 2-5. *Example of Metaballs*

Be careful with metaballs. When they get close to or interact with each other, they tend to blend or merge.

Text

Text creates text objects. It is active in Object mode and Edit mode.

Figure 2-6 shows a text object.

Figure 2-6. *Example of text*

Grease Pencil

Grease Pencil is active in Object mode, Edit mode, Sculpt mode, Draw mode, and Weight Paint mode. Blender objects allow you to draw in a 3D space. This acts as a container of strokes that you can create using drawing tools in Draw mode.

Figure 2-7 shows a Grease Pencil example.

Figure 2-7. *Example of the Grease Pencil*

Armature

Armature is active in Object mode, Edit mode, and Pose mode. It is designed to be posed in a static or an animated scene; they have a specific state called *rest position*.

Figure 2-8 shows an armature.

Figure 2-8. *Armature*

Lattice

Lattice is active in Object mode and Edit mode. It consists of a three-dimensional non-renderable grid of vertices and its main use is to apply a deformation to the object it controls with a Lattice modifier. The lattice should be scaled and moved to fit around your object in Object mode. Any scaling applied in Edit mode results in object deforming. It should also be noted that if the object is parented with Lattice deform, a Lattice modifier is automatically applied.

Figure 2-9 shows how Lattice works.

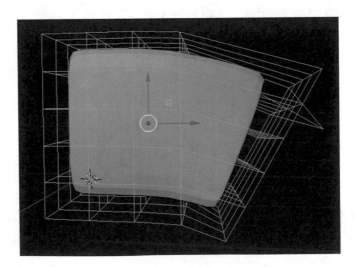

Figure 2-9. *Lattice at work*

Empty

Object mode is the only active mode. Empty is a single coordinate point with no additional geometry. Because Empty has no volume and surface, it can be rendered or used for other purposes.

Figure 2-10 shows examples of empties.

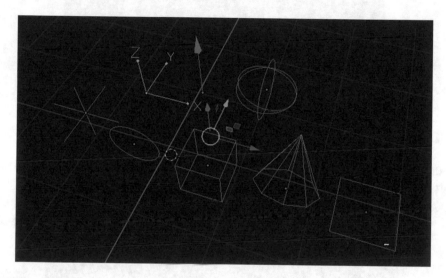

Figure 2-10. *Empties*

Image

Image is only in Object mode. It is usually used if you want to use an image as a reference.

Light

Light is only Object mode. It defines the light settings.

Figure 2-11 shows examples of lights.

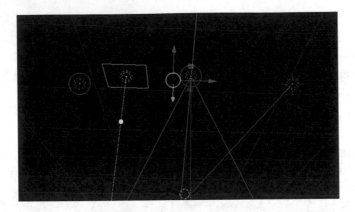

Figure 2-11. *Lights*

Light Probe

Only Object mode. It is used by Eevee as a support object. It records lighting information locally to light the scene using indirect lighting.

Figure 2-12 shows an example of light probes.

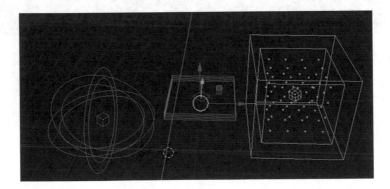

Figure 2-12. *Light Probes*

Camera and Speaker

Both only have Object mode. Camera is an object that provides a means of rendering images from Blender while Speaker provides sound in the 3D Viewport.

Figure 2-13 shows these objects.

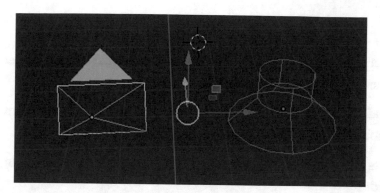

Figure 2-13. *Camera at the left, Speaker at the right*

Force Field

Object mode and Edit mode are the once active. It offers a way to influence a simulation; for example, to add extra movement. Force fields automatically affect everything.

Figure 2-14 shows examples of Force Field.

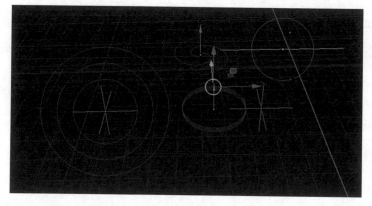

Figure 2-14. *Force Field samples*

Note   If you become confused by my listing objects that you can use to create your scene, there is a thin difference between a mesh and an object. A mesh is a surface defined by vertices, edges, and faces. Objects are more complex. They can be meshes, cameras, lights, light probes, and so forth. A mesh cannot become an object.

There are a lot of objects here. I discuss it soon, but let's proceed to the **menus**.

Menus

There are different types of menus: header menus, collapsing menus, select menus, popover menus, context menus, specials menus, and pie menus.

- **Header menus:** Located at the start of the header, they configure the editor and access tools.

- **Collapsing menus:** Helpful for gaining extra horizontal space in the header.

- **Select menus:** Lets you choose between a set of options.

- **Pop-over menus:** Overlay menus; includes the down arrow on the right side of menu button.

- **Context menus:** Pop-ups opened using right-click mouse button.

- **Special menus:** Contains a context-sensitive list of operators. It is opened by a button with a down arrow on dark background.

- **Pie menus:** Items are spread radially around the mouse.

Figure 2-15 shows examples of the Select menu, Header menu, Special menu, and Context menu.

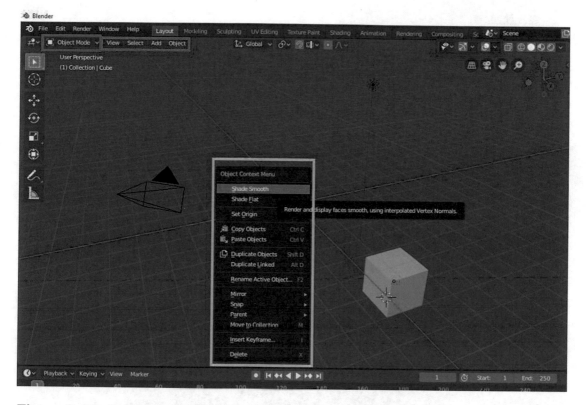

Figure 2-15. *Select menu (green), Header menus (yellow), Special menus (red), Context menu (light blue)*

The Mode selection under the File, Edit, and Render Header menus is called a Select menu. The Context menu that you can see in the middle of Figure 2-15 only shows when you right-click the space on your screen, but you can only do this if your mouse preference is set to left-click and you didn't change it to right-click.

View, Select, Add, and Object are examples of Header menus while the one inside the red rectangle which is under the Compositing tab are the examples of Special menus.

Figure 2-16 shows examples of the Collapse menu and Pop-over menu.

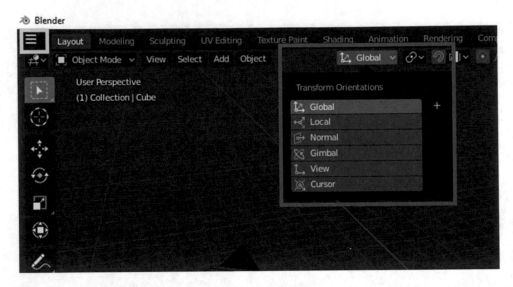

Figure 2-16. *Collapse menu and pop-over menu*

Figure 2-17 shows an example of the Pie menu.

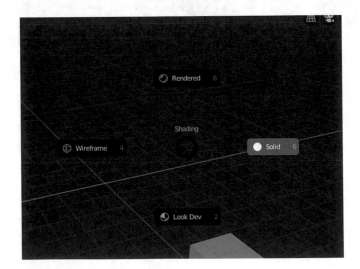

Figure 2-17. *Pie menu*

So, let's discuss each tools of the most commonly used workspace.

The Layout Workspace

The Layout workspace shows after the splash screen by default. This workspace contains a 3D Viewport editor in the top-left corner, Outliner in the top-right corner, Properties in the bottom-right corner, and the Timeline editor in the bottom-left corner.

Figure 2-18 shows the Layout workspace.

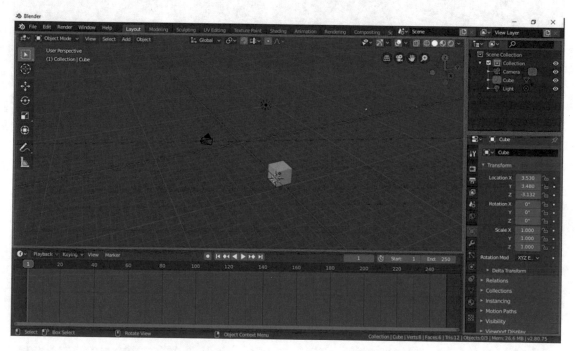

Figure 2-18. *Layout workspace*

Inside the brown rectangle is the 3D Viewport. The one inside the red rectangle is the Timeline Editor, the one in the yellow square is the Outliner, and the one in the green rectangle is the Properties.

The 3D Viewport

The 3D Viewport allows you to interact with a 3D scene for a variety of purposes, such as modeling, animating, texturing, painting, and so forth.

3D Viewport has three regions: Header, Toolbar, and Sidebar.

Figure 2-19 shows the layout of 3D Viewport.

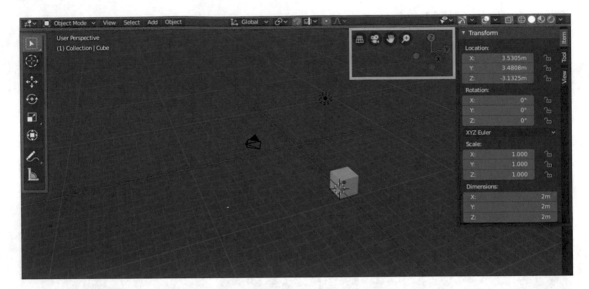

Figure 2-19. *3D Viewportlayout: Header (yellow), Gizmos (pink), Sidebar (red) and Toolbar (green)*

Header is also divided into three types: Mode and menus, Transform Control and Display and Shading. Gizmos are part of the Display and Shading. First, let's discuss the modes and menus.

3D Viewport ➤ Mode and Menus

Modes and menus consist of Select menu for modes and menus, which varies by the mode and object currently selected. Let's take a quick look at every menu in each mode in every object.

- **Mesh**
    - Object mode: View, Select, Add, Object
    - Edit mode: View, Select, Add, Mesh, Vertex, Edge, Face, UV
    - Sculpt mode: View, Sculpt, Brush, Hide/Mask
    - Vertex Paint: View, Paint, Brush
    - Weight Paint: View, Weights, Brush
    - Texture Paint: View, Brush

- **Curves**
  - Object mode: View, Select, Add, Object
  - Edit mode: View, Select, Add, Curve, Control Points, Segments
- **Surface**
  - Object mode: View, Select, Add, Object
  - Edit mode: View, Select, Add, Surface, Control Points, Segments
- **Metaballs**
  - Object mode: View, Select, Add, Object
  - Edit mode: View, Select, Add, Metaball
- **Text**
  - Object mode: View, Select, Add, Object
  - Edit mode: View, Edit, Font
- **Grease Pencil**
  - Object mode: View, Select, Add, Object
  - Edit mode: View, Select, Strokes
  - Sculpt mode: View, Select
  - Draw mode: View, Strokes
  - Weight Paint: View, Weights
- **Armature**
  - Object mode: View, Select, Add, Object
  - Edit mode: View, Select, Add, Armature
  - Pose mode: View, Select, Pose
- **Lattice**
  - Object mode: View, Select, Add, Object
  - Edit mode: View, Select, Lattice

- **Empty, Light, Light Probes, Camera, Speaker, and Force Field**

  - Object mode: View, Select, Add, Object

As you can see on the list, when it comes to Object mode, they have the same menus but it changes when it comes to the other modes, which by the name of the menu, you already have an idea about the tools. Let's first discuss the four common menus in Object mode: View, Select, Add, and Object.

What you see in these four menus are the same in whatever objects you are in; the exception is that when you currently select Metaball, Text, Lattice, Empty, Light, Light Probe, Camera, Speaker, or Force Field, the Join under Object Header menu is disabled.

Note   Shortcut keys are also indicated at the right side of the name of the command in the menus.

View Menu

The View menu is available at all six modes of 3D View editor with the same set of commands. By default, the toolbar is enabled while the sidebar and tool settings are disabled.

Figure 2-20 shows the toolbar, sidebar, and tool settings after being activated in the View menu.

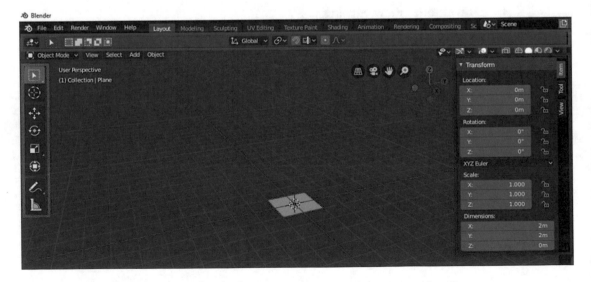

Figure 2-20. *Toolbar (yellow), Tool setting (violet), Sidebar (red)*

What you see in toolbar depends on the mode and workspace. The Object mode in the Layout workspace includes Select, Cursor, Move, Rotate, Scale, Transform, Annotate, and Measure. There is a rectangle on the side of Select, Scale, and Annotate. It is a pop-up menu for tools. This indicates more options for the tool. I discuss this more soon. For now, let's focus on the commands that we can see in the menus.

The Tool settings, as you can see in Figure 2-20, is a bar that holds some of the commonly used tools, like Transform Controls. The arrow inside the box represents the Select tool, and the five small icons beside it are for Selection mode. From left to right, you can

- Set a new selection

- Extend an existing selection

- Subtract an existing selection

- Invert an existing selection

- Intersect an existing selection

Let's discuss the Sidebar region, which consists of panels. For 3D Viewport, the sidebar consists of three panels. For now, let's discuss some of the commands under the View menu.

Adjust last operation are a set of operations that appear after modifying an object, like after using the rotate tool on a cube. Figure 2-21 shows how this works.

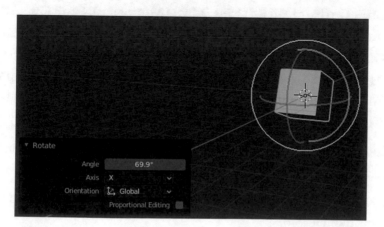

Figure 2-21. *Adjust Last Operation at work*

Frame Selected (Numpad.) and **Frame All** (Numpad Home key) are for zooming in on an object. If you select one or two objects, use Frame Selected. If you want to zoom in all objects in the scene, use **Frame all**.

Perspective/Orthographic (Numpad 5) changes the view of the scene. Orthographic is commonly used in engineering to produce objects specifications that communicate dimensions unambiguously appear to have same length everywhere on the drawing. This allows the drafter to dimension only a subset of lines and let the reader know that other lines of that length on the drawing are also that length in reality; however, with perspective mode lines of identical real-world lengths appear different due to fore-shortening. It becomes difficult to judge relative dimensions and size of objects in the distance.

- **Local view** (Numpad /) is to view a selected object in isolation mode. It is more effective if you have a lot of objects in the scene and you only need to modify one or two objects in it.

- **Cameras** (Numpad 0) activates your camera in View mode.

- **Viewpoint** is where you can set the different views for your project. You can have it in Top view (Numpad 7), Bottom view (Ctrl+Numpad 7), Front (Numpad 1), Back (Ctrl+Numpad 1), Right (Numpad 3), and Left (Ctrl+Numpad 3).

- **Navigation** includes Orbit Left (Numpad 4), Orbit Right (Numpad 6), Orbit Up (Numpad 8), Orbit Down (Numpad 2), Orbit Opposite (Numpad 9), Roll Left (Shift+Numpad 4), Roll Right (Shift+Numpad 6), Pan Left (Ctrl+Numpad 4), Pan Right (Ctrl+Numpad 6), Pan Up (Ctrl+Numpad 8), Pan Down (Ctrl+Numpad 2), Zoom In (Numpad +), Zoom Out (Numpad -), Zoom Border (Shift+B), Zoom Camera 1:1, Fly Navigation, and Walk Navigation.

- Under Navigation is **Align View**, where you can set the alignment of your view.

- **View Regions** is where you can set which part of your scene is only rendered or viewed.

- **Play Animation** is where you can render an image exactly as shown in the 3D Viewport.

- **Viewport Render Animation** is covered in Chapter 5, where I discuss play animation and viewport render animation.

- In **Area**, you can choose how to work in your workspace. There are six options: Toggle Quad View (Ctrl+Alt+Q), Horizontal split, Vertical split, Duplicate Area into New Window, Toggle Maximize Area (Ctrl+spacebar), and Toggle Full Screen (Ctrl+Alt+spacebar).

Select Menu

Let's talk about the **Select menu**. For the **Mesh object**, the Select menu is quite different when in Object mode and when in Edit mode. It also depends on the object that is currently selected.

Figure 2-22 shows the difference of the Select menu in Object mode and in Edit mode.

Figure 2-22. *Select menu, Edit mode and Object mode*

As you can see in Figure 2-22, if you want to select all of the objects in the scene, you need to click A on your keyboard and Alt+A to disable the selection. Press Ctrl+I if you want to invert the selection that currently have. It is easier than going to the Select menu. All are working in Object mode and in Edit mode.

In Edit mode, there is **Checker Deselect**, which deselects vertices, edges, or faces in checker style, as you can see in Figure 2-23.

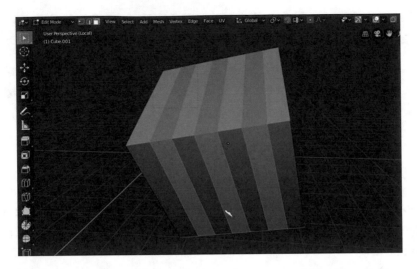

Figure 2-23. *Checker Deselect at work*

Let's talk about Object mode. **Select All by Type** is where you can select objects base on what type it is. This is useful if you have a lot of different kind of objects in the scene. This kind of tool is helpful in large productions.

Let's talk about the Select menu for other objects.

The common tools under the Select menu in Edit mode under **all objects** are All (A), None (Alt+A), Invert (Ctrl+I), Box Select (Tweak Left) and Circle Select (C). Let's discuss what the other tools in the Select menu of each object.

The following are under the Select menu for the **Armature object**.

- **Mirror** (Shift+Ctrl+M) mirrors the bone selection.

- **More** (Ctrl+Numpad +) selects the bones connected to the initial selection.

- **Less** (Ctrl+Numpad -) deselects the bones at the boundary of each selection region.

- **Parent** ([ ) and **Child** ( ]) select a bone's immediate parent/children.

- **Extend Parent** (Shift+[) and **Extend Child** (Shift+]) select the selected bone's immediate parent/children.

- **Similar** (Shift+G) selects bones by property type.

- **Select Pattern** selects objects matching a naming pattern.

The following are under the Select menu for the **Lattice** object.

- **Select Mirror** selects mirrored lattice points.

- **Select Random** randomly selects UVW (UV Unwarp) control points.

- **Select More** selects a vertex directly linked to selected ones.

- **Select Less** deselects vertices at the boundary of each selection region.

- **Ungrouped Verts** selects vertices without a group.

The following are under the Select menu for the **Metaball** object.

- **Select Random** randomly selects metaelements.

- **Similar** selects similar metaballs by property types.

The following are under the Select menu for the **Curve object**.

- **Select Random** randomly selects some control points,

- **Checker Deselect** deselects every other vertex,

- **Select Linked** (Ctrl+L) selects all control points linked to the current selection.

- **Select Similar** (Shift+G) selects similar curve points by property type.

- **(De)Select First/Last** deselects or selects first/last of visible part of each NURBS.

- **Select Next/Previous** selects points following/preceding the selected ones along the curves.

- **Select More** (Ctrl+Numpad +) selects control points directly linked to the selected ones.

- **Select Less** (Ctrl+Numpad -) reduces current selection by deselecting boundary elements.

The Select menu under **Surface object** has Select Random, Checker Deselect, Select Linked, Select Similar, Select More, and Select Less, which are the same as Curve. Let's discuss **Select Control Point Row** (Shift+R), which selects a row of control points including active one.

The following are under the Select menu for the **Stroke** object.

- **Linked** (L) selects all points in same strokes as the selected points.

- **Alternated** (Shift+L) selects alternative points in same strokes as the selected strokes.

- **Grouped** (Shift+G) selects all strokes with similar characteristics.

- **Select First/Select Last** selects first/last point in Grease Pencil.

- **Select More/Less** (Ctrl+Numpad+/Ctrl+Numpad -) grow/shrinks sets of selected Grease Pencil points.

Note   Camera, Speaker, Empty, Force Field, and Light Probe only have the Select menu (see Figure 2-22).

Add Menu

The Add menu has different options for different modes at the same time for different objects where it is available.

Figure 2-24 shows the comparison of the Add menu from Object mode to Edit mode and the Add menus from different objects.

Figure 2-24. *Add menu in Object mode (left) Add menu in Edit mode (center and right)*

As you can see in Figure 2-25, the add menu in Object mode contains the **list of all the objects** available for you to use while the one in Edit mode is the **list of options** available for the current object selected. If you have object selected, and you go to Edit mode and add an object, the two objects are counted as one when you go back to Object mode (unlike when you add an object while you're in Object mode, they considered separate objects).

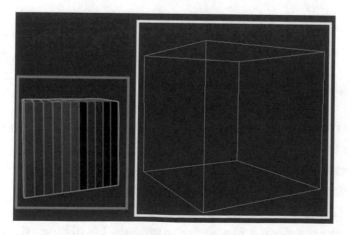

Figure 2-25. *Mesh box (left) and Texture Space (right)*

The Mesh, Vertex, Edge, Face, and UV header menus are in Edit mode under the Mesh object. Most of them are straightforward; the Blender docs explain anything that you are unsure about.

The most noteworthy options are under Transform Move Texture Space and Scale Texture Space, which move/scale texture space.

Figure 2-25 shows texture space.

Texture space is the space that holds or controls your texture. By default, it is attached in the object, like skin to a body. Be careful scaling or moving this because it affects the output of your texture in your mesh or any objects applied by textures.

Most of the tools under the Mesh, Edge, Vertex, and Face menus are on the Modeling workspace toolbar. The one under the UV menu is on the UV toolbar for the UV workspace.

Object Menu

The last menu that I discuss is the Object menu. It is in the Object mode for all types of objects and consists of tools that are used for manipulating objects. You can take it as a long way of manipulating objects since we already have toolbars.

There are other header menus that I didn't discuss, but their commands are advanced. Let's discuss Transform Controls, which are part of the Header region.

3D Viewport ➤ Transform Controls

These are set of tools for easily transform or modify your scene. Figure 2-26 shows the sets of tools.

Figure 2-26. *Transform Control tools*

At the left are the pop-over menus for Transform Orientation, Pivot Point, Snapping, and Proportional Edit.

Transform Orientation affects the behavior of the transformations: Locate, Rotate, and Scale. The effect is seen on object manipulators, as well as on transformation constraints, Axis Locking.

Global bases the transformation on the world axis. **Local** bases the transformation on the object selected. When you choose **Normal**, the transformation matches the normal of the object selected. For beginners, normal is a direction or line that is perpendicular to something—typically, a triangle or a surface, but it can also be relative to a line, a tangent line for a point on a curve, or a tangent plane for a point on a surface.

Normal states the direction in which an object should face. For example, when you are applying hair particles on your meshes, you need to make sure that the normals are facing upward. Figure 2-27 shows an example of a normal. The ones sticking out of the corners are the normals of the edges and vertices of the cube. There are also normals for faces.

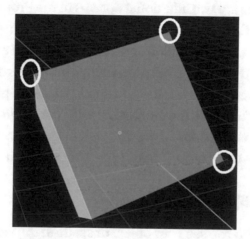

Figure 2-27. *Example of normals in meshes*

Now, let's go back to the Transform Orientations. **Gimbal** uses the Gimbal behavior that changes depending on the current rotation mode. Gimbal is a pivoted support that allows the rotation of an object about a single axis.

View matches its transformation of the 3D Viewport.

With the **Cursor, the** transformation matches the current defined 3D cursor in the Blender.

The **Pivot Point** tool allows you to choose the location of the origin point. Depending on your project, changing the location of the pivot point or the origin point helps you easily manipulate your objects.

The **Snapping** tool gives you the ability to snap objects and meshes to various types of scene elements during a transformation. **Increment** snaps to grid points, and when you are in orthographic view, the snapping increment changes depending on zoom level. **Vertex** snaps to vertices of mesh objects. **Edge** snaps the edge of a mesh object. **Face snaps** the face of a mesh objects. **Volume** snaps to regions within the volume of the first object found below the mouse cursor. This one controls the depth of the transformed element.

The last thing I'd like to discuss in 3D Viewport is the **Proportional Editing** tool, which transforms selected elements (such as vertices) and nearby elements. For example, the movement of a single vertex causes the movement of unselected vertices within a given range. Since proportional editing affects the nearby geometry, it is very useful when you need to smoothly deform the surface of a dense mesh. This tool is typically used in Edit mode but it can also be used in Object mode.

You can see that there are two additional options in the Proportional Editing tool in Edit mode, which are Connected Only and Projected from View. When you use **Connected Only,** the proportional falloff spreads via geometry rather than using a radius only. This means that you can proportionally edit the vertices in a finger of a hand without affecting the other fingers. While the other vertices are physically close in 3D space, they are far away following the topological edge connections of the mesh. If you use **Projected From View,** the depth along the view is ignored when applying the radius.

Let's now discuss the Display and Shading part of the Header region.

3D Viewport ➤ Display and Shading

These tools affect how you can see your object or scene in the viewport. These set of tools consists of Object Type Visibility, Viewport Gizmos, X-Ray, Viewport Overlays, and Viewport Shading.

Figure 2-28 shows these tools closely.

Figure 2-28. *Display and Shading tools*

In the **Object Type Visibility** pop-over menu, the visibility and selectability per type of object can be specified or limited per 3D Viewport. The eye icon beside each object types limits the visibility while the arrow icon limits the selectability. This tool is more efficient for a large production where you have many objects to manipulate.

As you can see in Figure 2-29, the objects are Mesh, Curve, Surface, Meta (Metaball), Text, Grease Pencil, Armature, Lattice, Empty, Light, Light Probe, Camera, and Speaker.

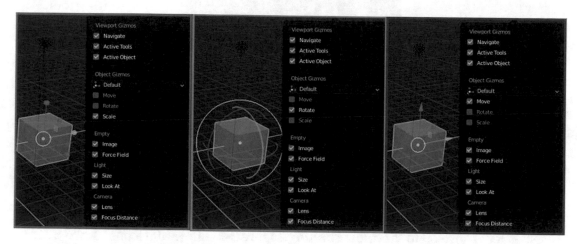

Figure 2-29. *Gizmos at work*

Next is **Gizmos**. This pop-up menu helps you easily manipulate the settings for some of your tools. It is a bounding box used for manipulating 3D objects. What you can see in this pop-up menu is more on enabling/disabling the basic tools in the 3D Viewport, like move, rotate and scale. When you do move, rotate, and scale an object, there is an arrow pointing the x, y, and z axis, as shown in Figure 2-29. By default, they are disabled, but you can move the object by using a hotkey like Rotate, which is R, or Scale, which is S, or move, which is G, and press the axis letter so that it transforms consistently to the axis you want. For example, if you want to move along the x axis, press G, and then X; the movement is activated only along the x axis.

As you can see in Figure 2-29, when you enable the scale under Object Gizmos, there are three arrows showing in the cube pointing toward different direction. One to the x axis, one to the y axis, the other one is to the z axis. This is the same when you enable the move function except that there is difference in the tip of the arrow. In scale, the tip of the arrow is in square while in the move the tip of the arrow is in cube. When you enable rotate, a half-circle indicates a turn in direction. This is how Object Gizmos work, but we also have Viewport Gizmos. What are they and how do they work?

If you notice the x, y, z that seems for navigation in the top-right part of the 3D Viewport editor, that one is part of Viewport Gizmos. Figure 2-30 shows these tools.

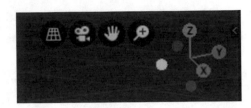

Figure 2-30. *Viewport Gizmos: Navigate*

The one shown in Figure 2-30 is the Gizmos for Navigation. This feature helps you to easily navigate in the viewport, especially for laptop users (like me) or beginners still learning the hotkeys to navigate the 3D Viewport. I can say that this new feature is quite helpful.

Let's talk about **Viewport Overlays.** This pop-over menu is also for disabling/enabling tools regarding things for modeling like

Now, let's move on to **Viewport Shading**. Figure 2-31 shows the icons that represent Viewport Shading tools.

Figure 2-31. *Left to right: Show X-Ray, Viewport Shading, Wireframe, Solid, LookDev, Rendered*

Show X-Ray is the overlapping square icon. It renders the scene as transparent, as shown in Figure 2-32.

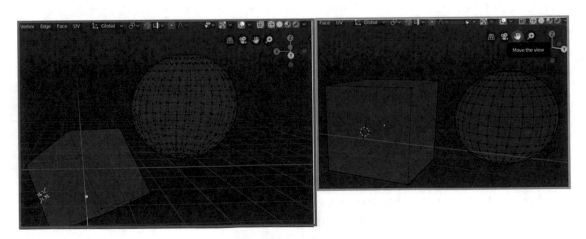

Figure 2-32. *Viewport Shading: Show X-Ray plus Wireframe in Edit mode (left) and Viewport Shading: Wireframe only in Edit mode*

In Figure 2-32, the difference when you use the Show X-Ray or Transparency tool. Where Show X-Ray is active, you can see the other side of the sphere and cube. On the right side, you can only see the side of the object facing the screen. This feature can help you easily select vertices, edges or faces without accidentally selecting the vertices, edges or faces from the other side of an object.

Let's proceed to the **Wireframe mode**, which is the first circle beside the Show X-Ray. This mode shows the full scene by only displaying the edges and vertices of the objects. Figure 2-33 shows the settings that you can adjust in this mode.

Figure 2-33. *Viewport Shading: Wireframe mode setting*

In Figure 2-33, you can change the color, background, set the X-Ray visibility, and change the color outline.

- Let's talk about **Color**. When you choose single, the scene color was based to a single color only. When you choose object, it shows the object color and when you choose random, it randomly chooses a color.

- Let's talk about **Background**. When you choose Theme, what you set in the User Preference is used in the background. When you choose World, whatever the setting is in the World scene is used as the background. Take note that the world scene has its own lighting so be careful on the color you choose for this part. You also better check its setting before applying this as your background. When you choose viewport, whatever settings you have for the viewport are the ones to use.

- Let's talk about **X-Ray**. We know in laboratory tests X-rays show what's inside of a body. It's the same for this feature. When you adjust the X-Ray value to a higher value, the more you can see what is inside of an object.

- Let's talk about **Outline**. The outline means the sides of the object. You can change it to the color you want to emphasize the sides of the objects. You can also use this to know the silhouette of the 3D model you are making, if it matches the idea you have in mind.

In **Solid mode**, there are three options for lighting: the Studio, MatCap, and Flat. In this mode, it is the default view of your scene when you are modeling. You can easily see what your mesh looks like after you modify it.

- **MatCap** usually used for sculpting for you to clearly see the shadows of your meshes and this kind of lighting use a material capture to light the objects in the scene.

- **Flat** does not calculate any lighting, which is why Figure 2-42 is too bright and there are no shadows.

- In **Studio**, a shadow isn't that visible unlike in MatCap. This kind of setting use studio lights to light objects and this kind of lights can follow camera or be fixed.

Figure 2-34 shows the Studio, MatCap, and Flat settings at work.

Figure 2-34. *Studio, MatCap, and Flat at work*

We can see in Figure 2-34 the differences of the three lightings. In Flat, it was too bright. You can't see any shadows at all while in Studio, shadow isn't that visible unlike in MatCap. But since this can only be seen in view mode and is not seen in the actual render of an image, this might help you in some way.

Before I proceed to the next shading mode, I'd like to briefly discuss this **Backface Culling.** What is Backface Culling? Backface Culling is an important part of how a 3D software or engine determines whether a polygon of a graphical object is visible. It is a step in a graphical pipeline that tests whether the points in the polygon appear in counter-clockwise or clockwise order when projected in the screen. If not visible, the polygon is culled from rendering process, which increases efficiency by reducing the number of polygons that the hardware has to draw.

That's all for that topic. Now let's look at the enhanced Material Preview, which is the **LookDev mode**. This mode is located beside the solid mode. Coming from the left side, it is the third circle. In Figure 2-35, you can see what it looks like.

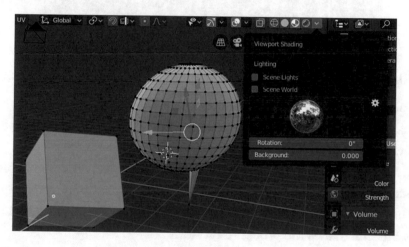

Figure 2-35. *Viewport Shading: LookDev mode*

LookDev mode, or Look Development mode, is the enhanced version of Material Preview from 2.7 version of Blender. They said this mode is the equivalent of Material Preview with better shading and more advance features so for me, I'd like to introduce it as the enhanced version of the Material Preview. It is the same. In this mode, you can see how your material works in your meshes, as shown in Figure 2-35. You can see the shadow and lighting at work but the lighting is not native lighting or the lighting you use in your scenes, instead it overrides scenes lamps and scene world with a generic user configurable environment lighting, which is more neutral on your materials and quicker to render.

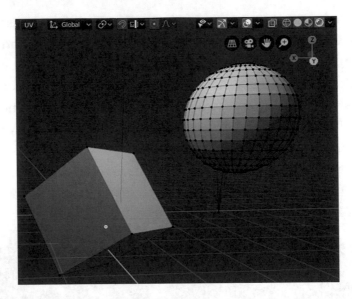

Figure 2-36. *Viewport Shading: Render mode*

In the LookDev settings, there are two options for lighting: the Scene Lights and Scene World. When you activate the **Scene Light**, you see how your lighting in the scenes affects your materials. The lamp you choose or sun, whatever lighting you have in your scene. If you choose **Scene World**, you see is the effect of the light coming from the World Scene. You can also change the direction of your lighting by changing the **Rotation.** This means you can also use your scene lamps or scene world lighting to test in LookDev. But that makes the process a bit slower.

Let's now move to the last Shading display, the Render mode. In this mode, you can see what your project looks like in the final render. You can check the mesh, materials, and lighting, as you can see in Figure 2-36.

Figure 2-36 shows lighting at work and material at Render view mode. It does seem a little similar with LookDev but in LookDev, by default, scene lighting and scene world are not used for faster performance, for instant previews and more responsive editing. There are pause button that appears beside the Viewport Shading tools for you to be able to pause or cancel the rendering process.

3D Viewport ➤ Toolbar

The shortcut key for activating tools in the toolbar is spacebar + <the tool's shortcut key>. These tools are quite helpful because not all beginners can easily adapt to software user interface and shortcuts but if they are familiar with some tools, they can at least easily get started.

Figure 2-37 shows the set of tools available in the Layout workspace.

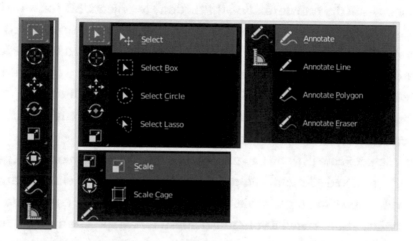

Figure 2-37. *Toolbar for Layout workspace (left) and Available options for Select, Scale and Annotate (center and right)*

When you look closely in Select, Scale and Annotate icons, you can see a small triangle. This indicates that there are other options for the tool. On the left side of the figure, there are the other options for the three tools.

Let's discuss the tools. There are four tools under the Select Box pop-up menu: **Select** (W), **Select Box** (B), **Select Circle** (C), and **Select Lasso** (L). The Select tool simply selects an element. Select Box tool selects boxes. Select Circle is for circle selection. Select Lasso selects items using Lasso tool. Lasso tool don't have specific shape when selecting items. Once you click on a space or an element to start the selection, you need to drag the mouse cursor for the selection and it automatically selects or deselects elements around the scene, as shown in Figure 2-38.

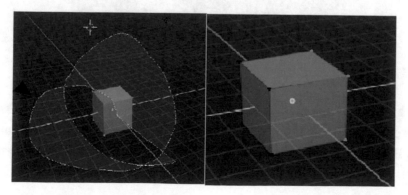

Figure 2-38. *Select Lasso tool at work*

Under You Select tool is the **Cursor tool** (spacebar), which is used for editing for indicating the basis of the transformation that is done to objects. 3D software like Blender works through a lot of calculations and formulas. For example, in order to scale an object, the program needs to know the basis of the scale computation. As in our Geometry subject, we cannot completely solve a problem without a given variable. This is the same with the 3D software. That is the reason we have this cursor tool. Pivot Point is to let the program know the given location of the object for its transformation.

Let's discuss the **Scale tool**, which also has a pop-up menu.

When you select **Scale** (S), you can only scale based on the cursor, pivot point, or center point of a selected element. **Scale cage** (3) cages a selected element and adds a point there, which you can drag to scale. Figure 2-39 shows a scale cage when it works. Both have benefits. Scale is used if your mesh doesn't have specific details to scale and for faster processes, like architectural design. Most architectural design doesn't have much detail, unlike game environment designs.

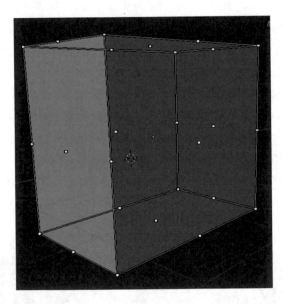

Figure 2-39. *Scale Cage at work*

As you can see in Figure 2-39, there are white points in the edges and corners of the mesh that is currently working on. That is the Scale Cage tool at work. You can scale the edge corner in the direction you wanted without affecting the other edge corner unlike in scale only.

The **Annotate** tool has four tools under it: **Annotate** (5) creates a simple note; **Annotate Line** (6) creates a note that uses a line; **Annotate Polygon** (7) is the same as Annotate Line but you can click the space, and it automatically creates a line while right-clicking the space to stop it; and **Annotate Eraser** (8) erases the annotation.

The Annotation hotkey is spacebar+D since the spacebar is the default hotkey for accessing any tools in the toolbar. But when you click the Annotate tool, the Annotate tool hotkey changes from D to 5. Changes to Annotate hotkeys affect other hotkeys, so be aware.

Under Scale tool is the **Measure** tool (M). This tool can measure more than lines. It also does angles by dragging up the middle portion of the line formed by the measuring tool. If you want to delete the measurement you created, you need to select it and press X in the keyboard or by clicking another tool. It also should be noted that to create new measurement, you need to tweak left anywhere, drag ruler segment to measure an angle and hold Shift while dragging to measure surface thickness.

Figure 2-40 shows how the Measure tool works.

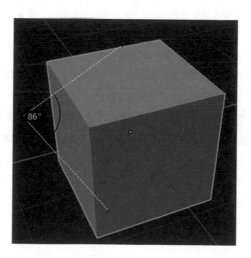

Figure 2-40. *Measure at work*

3D Viewport ➤ Sidebar

The Sidebar region is the panel that you can see the right part of your 3D Viewport editor when it is activated in the View menu or when you press N in your keyboard. Sidebar consists of three default tabs: Item, Tool, and View. In the **Item tab**, you can see the actual values of the location, rotation, scale, and dimensions of an object. You can also use this tab to modify those properties of an object. In the **Tool tab**, you see the currently active tool displayed, as well as other settings related to the active tool, as shown in Figure 2-41.

Figure 2-41. *Select tool activated and shown in Sidebar ➤ Tool panel*

In Figure 2-41, aside from the active Select Box tool, you can see the selection modes in the Tool panel.

You can also see the current workspace in the Workspace panel. The **View tab** is where you adjust the camera settings and the 3D cursor settings.

The Sidebar

Before I talk about the other editors in the Layout workspace, let me talk about the Status Bar.

This bar is at the bottom of your screen. It is helpful especially when you want to know about shortcuts, the number of vertices/faces that you currently have, or the amount of memory your computer has used while working on your current project. It also gives suggestions on what to do while you're taking an action, which can be very handy.

Outliner

Outliner is a list that organizes data in the Blend file, like scene data, video sequencer data, or anything that is stored in a Blend file. It is used to view the data in a scene, select and deselect objects, hide or show an object, enable or disable the selection, enable or disable rendering or an object, delete objects, or unlink data.

Figure 2-42 shows this data editor.

Figure 2-42. *Outliner*

Figure 2-42 shows the active objects. You can filter the objects and the arrangement of your objects through the settings under the funnel icon; but that setting is only available in Outliner, in Layout workspace. You can also create new collection by clicking the shoebox-like icon with a plus beside the filter setting.

Let's now proceed to the Properties Editor.

Properties

Properties editor shows and allows editing of many active data, including the active scene and object. It has several categories, which are chosen via tabs. What you can see in properties depends on the current object selected, as you can see in Figure 2-43. Let's first discuss the general categories.

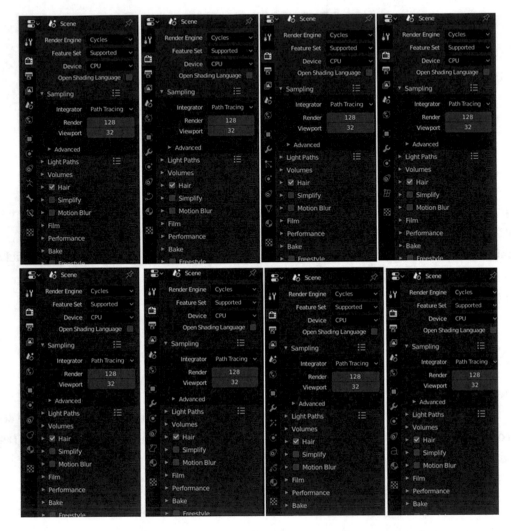

Figure 2-43. *Properties (Top Left ➤ Right: Armature, Curve, Mesh, Lattice; Bottom Left ➤ Right: Metaball, Surface, Grease Pencil and Text)*

What you can see in the Active tool and Workbench settings in the properties is the same as what you can see in the tool panel of Sidebar. It displays the current active tool of the toolbar and the other settings related to the tool.

Now, we let's discuss the Render settings that fall under scene settings.

Render Settings

Blender 2.80 has three built-in render engines: Eevee, Cycles, and Workbench. Eevee is Blender's real-time render engine built using OpenGL focused on speed and interactivity while achieving the goal of rendering PBR materials.

- **Eevee** is used interactively in the 3D Viewport but also produce high-quality final renders but unlike Cycles, it is not a raytrace render engine. Instead of computing each of ray light, it uses a process called rasterization, which estimates the way light interacts with objects and materials using numerous algorithms.

- **Cycles** is Blender's physically-based path tracer for production rendering. It is designed to provide physically based results out-of-the-box, with artistic control and flexible shading nodes for production needs.

- **Workbench** is optimized for fast rendering during modeling and animation preview. It is not intended to be a render engine that renders final images for a project. Its primary task is to display a scene in the 3D Viewport when it is being worked on. It is noted that even though the Workbench engine is not intended to render final images/animation, it is also among the options in Render Engine.

By default, Cycle is the render engine that is selected in the options.

In Figure 2-44, the Workbench settings are the same as what you see in the viewport shading, except there are Sampling, Film, Simplify, and Color Management.

Figure 2-44. *Eevee, Cycles, and Workbench: Properties ➤ Render*

Eevee and Cycles both have Motion Blur, Hair, and Freestyle. The common settings for the three render engines are Sampling, Simplify, Film, and Color Management.

Sampling Settings

The setting of **Sampling** adjusts the samples per pixel that you can render or see in the viewport. Giving a high value of samples can give a high quality of rendering but also can slow down the rendering process, depends on your project.

- **Ambient Occlusion** is a method to approximate how bright light should be shining on any specific part of a surface, based on the light and its environment. Enabling it helps you add realism to your scene.

- **Bloom** is a post-process effect that diffuses very bright pixels. Enabling this one helps you manage the brightness of your scene.

- **Depth of field** is the distance between the nearest and the furthest objects that are in acceptably sharp focus in an image. This technique is used in photography.

- **Subsurface Scattering** is a mechanism of light transport in which light that penetrates the surface of a translucent object is scattered by interacting with the material and exits the surface at a different point. Just like Ambient Occlusion, this setting can help you add realism to your scene.

- **Screen Space Reflection** affects all materials and uses the depth buffer and the previous frame color to create more accurate reflection than reflection probes.

- **Motion Blur** creates the blurred effect in animation.

- **Volumetric** adds a lighting effect on your scene to allow you viewer to see beams of light shining through the environment.

- **Hair** is used when you have hair particles in your scene to give more effect to it.

- **Shadows** sets your scenes' shadows to give more effect and realism.

- **Indirect Lighting** sets your indirect lighting, like Light Probes. Here, you can bake your lighting and make additional adjustment for better view of your scene.

- **Film** adjusts things related to transparency or pixel setting of an image.

- **Simplify** sets the global maximum subdivision level and global child particles percentage during rendering and during its project's process in the viewport.

- **Color Management** adjusts the color or anything related to best display of an image or animation that is rendered.

- **Volumes** renders effects like fire, smoke, mist, absorption in glass, and many other effects that cannot be represented by surface meshes alone.

- **Light Paths** sets the number of light bounces.

- **Freestyle** draws stylized strokes and sets the thickness of the strokes.

- **Bake** manipulates the freezing and recording of the result of a computer process

You can see on the top part of the Cycles, there is this select menu for device. In Cycles, you can choose how to render your image, if you use your GPU or CPU to render it.

Note   GPU stands for *graphical processing unit*; it handles the visual elements. CPU stands for *central processing unit*, which handles the physical and logical elements of the computer.

Next, let's discuss the Output settings.

Output Settings

Output is where you can set what file extension or where your final image is saved. You can set the final color scheme if it is RGB, RGBA, or Black and White. You can set the compression of the image too.

In Figure 2-45, there's no difference in the settings of the three render engines.

- **Stereoscopy** allows the use of multiple views in the scene.

- **Metadata** is the data of the file or image. You can set the information you want your file to have when it was saved.

- **Post Processing** is the final processing. Adding a final effect to your image makes it look better.

Figure 2-45. *Eevee, Workbench, and Cycle: Properties ➤ Output*

View Layer Settings

View Layer is commonly used for compositing or post-processing process.

Cycles has additional settings for this category, as you can see in Figure 2-46. Eevee is on the bottom left of Figure 2-46 and Workbench on the top left.

Renders can be separated into layers. It is different from collections because collections are used for objects and layers are used for rendered images for post-processing.

Figure 2-46. *Workbench (top left), Eevee (bottom left) and Cycles (right):*
Properties ➤ View Layer

View Layer can save you from having to re-render your entire image each time you
change something, allowing you to instead re-render only the layer/s that you need,
which is useful in animation. Adding and removing layers is done in the settings, which
show the list of layers that you can see at the upper-right corner of your screen.

You can add layer by clicking the overlapping paper icon at the right. You can also
delete a layer by selecting the layer first and clicking the X icon. Note that the current
layer selected in this section is the layer that appears in View Layer under Properties.

Passes Settings

Under the **Passes** settings, Eevee and Cycles both have the following.

- **Combined** delivers fully combined RGBA buffers.

- **Z** delivers the Z value pass.

- **Mist** delivers mist factor pass.

- **Normal** delivers normal pass.

- **Ambient Occlusion** delivers an ambient occlusion pass.

What is Passes all about? Passes split rendered images into colors, direct and indirect light to edit them individually, and extracts data such as depth or normals.

Eevee's Passes settings include **Subsurface Direct,** which delivers a subsurface direct pass, and **Subsurface Color,** which delivers a subsurface color pass.

Cycles' settings in Passes include **Cryptomatte,** which is a standard to efficiently create mattes for compositing. Unlike in Material and Object index passes, the objects to isolate are selected in compositing, and mattes are anti-aliased, and take into account effects like motion blur and transparency.

Scene Settings

Now, let's proceed to the next category, which is **Scene.** All render engines have the same settings at this category.

Under the Scene panel, there is **Camera**, where you choose an active camera for rendering scene; **Background Scene**, where you set a background for your scene; and **Action Movie Clip**, where you set active movie clips for constraints and viewport drawing.

World Settings

The next category is **World,** where you can adjust everything that can affect your project. The world environment can emit light, ranging from a single solid color to arbitrary textures.

In World, the three render engines have differences. View Port Display and Custom Properties are common in the three render engines. In **Viewport Display**, you can change the color of the viewport but changes appear in Rendered Shading Viewport or after you render an image. These changes can also affect your image since the color that you set in Viewport Display can be treated as its background, as shown in Figure 2-47.

Figure 2-47. *Viewport Display at work under Rendered Shading Viewport and Workbench Engine*

Figure 2-48 shows the effect of Viewport Display on Eevee and Cycles Render Engine.

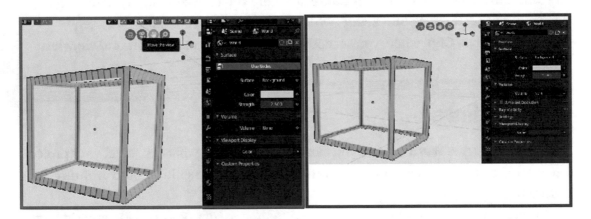

Figure 2-48. *Viewport display at work under Rendered Shading Viewport and Eevee (red) and Cycles (blue)*

The Viewport shading's color remains blue, the color of the background changes and become white which is the color indicated under the Surface panel. This means that for Eevee and Cycles, Surface's settings is based on the background color, not the viewport display.

Custom Properties is if you want to edit a property and this is quite too technical.

Eevee and Cycles both have Surface and Volume. Eevee has Use Nodes settings, which you cannot see in the Surface settings in Cycles.

Use Nodes in the Surface setting of Eevee enables you to use shaders for your World settings. When you disable this, the three options below it (Surface, Color, and Strength) are hidden.

Surface consists of the list of BSDF shaders that you can use for your World setting. **Color** consists of some shaders (like Texture Shaders, Input Shaders, Color Shaders, and Converter Shaders) that you can use for your World settings when you click the small circle beside the color picker. You can also change the color using the color picker. **Strength** is where you can adjust the strength of the impact of the color or shaders in the World settings. If you click the small circle beside the input box, you can see a lot of options that can help you improve your world settings.

The settings I discuss for Surface, Color, and Strength are seen in Eevee and Cycles.

Object Settings

Object is where you can adjust the things related to an object, like its location, rotation, scaling, object relations, collections, visibility, and so forth. The three render engines have the same settings for Object except that Cycles have Motion Blur. I'd like to note that in some objects, the motion blue setting in Cycles doesn't appear, such as when your current selected object is Light.

Transform, Relations, Collections, Instancing, Motion Paths, Visibility, Viewport Display, Custom Properties, and Motion Blur are exclusive to Cycles.

- **The Transform panel** is where you can move, scale, and rotate the selected object in exact value you wanted. You can even change the flow of the rotation through Rotation mode. Delta Transform is an extra data added to the object that is transformed.

- **The Relations panel** is where you can set the relationship between the objects. You can set which object is the parent or the basis of the transform that you will do in the scene.

- **The Collections panel** is where you can assign your object to an existing collection or even remove it from the collection. You can even create another collection from to be part of the object that is currently selected.

- **Instancing** helps you speed not only your modeling but also your rendering. Because what it does is duplicating your elements without duplicating the data it does have. What does it mean? Every object in the scene has its own data or properties. Duplicating the objects together with its properties make your GPU or CPU work a lot harder, ended up rendering slow. What's instancing does is to duplicate only the object, like cloning, without taking its properties.

- **Motion Paths** is used in animation. This setting is for paths that direct the objects on movement.

- **Visibility** sets the visibility and includes Ray Visibility. The object can only be seen in viewport but not in the renderer and other settings related to visibility.

- **Viewport display** helps you manipulate things related to the viewport, such as displaying the object name by enabling the **Name**; displaying the object's origin and axes in the viewport by enabling **Axis**; making the object draw in front of other objects by enabling **In front;** and setting how to display the object in the viewport in **Display As**.

- **Custom Properties** allows you to add and edit a property. It's an advanced topic.

Physics Settings

The three render engines have the same Physics settings, but this setting depends on the object currently selected.

The Physics system allows you to simulate a number of different real-world physical phenomena. You can use these systems to create a variety of static and dynamic effects such as rain, smoke, dust, water, cloth, and so forth. We tackle this more in Chapter 5 since this is part of animation.

Let's have a quick discussion about the other Properties categories.

Material Settings

Workbench has the fewest settings among the three because it is meant for modeling only. So, let's compare Cycles and Eevee, and look at some highlights.

- **Preview gives** a glimpse of what your material looks like before applying it to your mesh.

- **Surface is** where you edit your materials. There's a slight difference between Eevee and Cycles when it comes to this. Eevee has a Use Nodes button but Cycles doesn't. Cycles uses the BSDF list in the Select menu. Blender has its own Shader workspace.

- **Volume is** where you edit your material to add volume to it. It has the BSDF shader list.

- **Surface ➤ Multiple Importance** (Cycles) uses multiple importance sampling for the current material selected and disabling may reduce noise for large objects that emit little light compared to other light source.

- **Surface ➤ Transparent Shadows** (Cycles) uses transparent shadows for the current material selected if it contains a Transparent BSDF and disabling renders faster but does not give accurate shadows.

- **Volume ➤ Sampling** (Cycles) is where you can choose your sampling method for volume. There are three options: Multiple Importance, Distance, and Equiangular.

- **Volume ➤ Interpolation** (Cycles) is where you can choose interpolation method use for smoke/fire volume. There are two options: Linear and Cubic.

- **Volume ➤ Homogeneous** (Cycles) assumes the volume has the same density everywhere when using volume rendering for faster rendering process.

Note   BSDF stands for Bidirectional Scattering Distribution Function. It's a mathematical function that determines the probability of a specific ray of light reflecting at a given angle. If the shaders have a suffix BSDF, which means that the shader scatters light. We also have BSSRDF, which stands for Bidirectional Surface Scattering Reflectance Distribution Function; it is where materials don't simply reflect the light but absorbs it and then reflects it later.

Let's proceed to two categories that appear in all objects: Object Constraints and Texture.

Object Constraints and Texture Settings

In **Texture settings**, you can create textures for your scene, such as Blend, Clouds, Distorted Noise, Magic, Marble, Musgrave, Noise, Stucci, Voronoi, and Wood. You can also choose your own image to upload as normal texture. You can also see these options in the Shading workspace. What you can do here can also be done when you are in the Shading workspace or using the Shader Editor.

Object Constraints control an object's properties using either plain static values or another object. Even though constraints are useful in static projects, their main usage is in animation, so I discuss this more in Chapter 5.

Object Data modifies data for your object. The modifiers in the Layout workspace are a bit different from those in the Modeling workspace.

Sample Project Time!

Figures 2-49 to 2-73 show how to do a simple project in the Layout workspace.

Figure 2-49 shows adding a mesh.

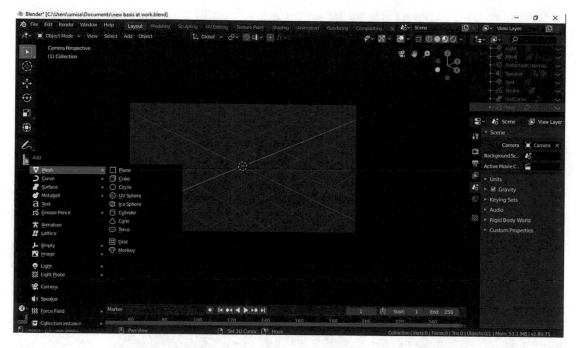

Figure 2-49. *Adding object, plane*

Press Shift+A to view the list of objects, proceed to Mesh, and choose Plane. Figure 2-49 is in camera perspective. To do that, you can go to View Menu ➤ Viewpoint ➤ Camera or press 0 on your numpad key.

Figure 2-50 shows how one of the transform tools rotates.

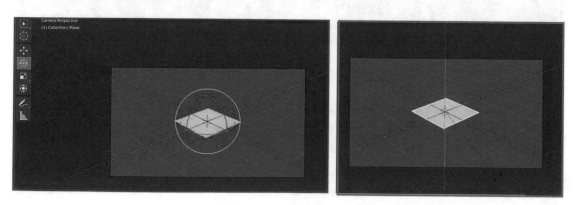

Figure 2-50. *Rotating plane object*

By default, plane object is lying flat on the grid of our 3D Viewport. As you click the Rotate tool, you can see three curves in green, red, and blue intersecting each other. Red means rotating in the x axis. Green means rotating in y axis and blue means rotating in z axis. There is also another technique in rotating your object. As you can see on the right side of Figure 2-50, there is a vertical blue line intersecting the plane. That is the z axis. This happens when you press R and then Z to indicate that you only rotate in the z axis. If you want to rotate in the x axis only, you can press X; press Y for the y axis.

In Figure 2-51, you see the next stage: adding materials.

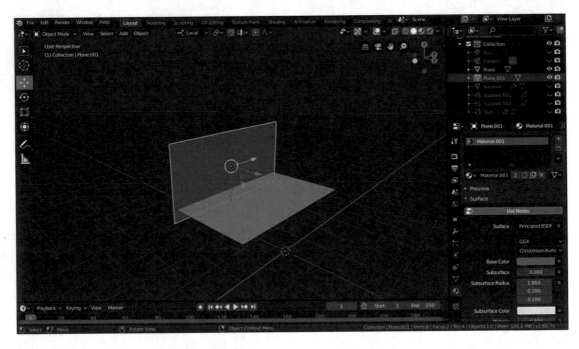

Figure 2-51. *Adding materials*

Add another plane to make a stage-like scene and add materials. Remember that you should do this in Object mode only so that you will appreciate the benefit of the Modeling workspace that we're about to discuss.

Figure 2-52 shows the Grease Pencil object at work. To add a Grease Pencil, you need to go to the Add menu ➤ Grease Pencil, and then click Suzanne; or press Shift+A, and then click the Grease Pencil and click Suzanne.

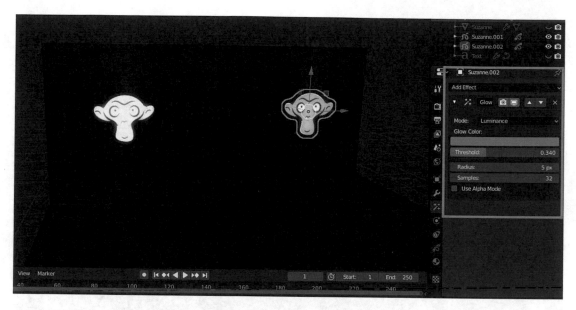

Figure 2-52. *Suzanne Grease Pencil at work*

Lighting is still disabled so that you can focus on the Grease Pencil. As you can see, you should add two Suzanne Grease Pencil and a glow effect in Luminance mode. The two Suzanne grease pencils should have a different glow color but they both have the following: Threshold of 0.340, Radius of 5px, and Samples of 32. By default, its radius is 50.

Now add some text. For the text object, you need to use the Edit mode in order to change text to Suzanne (see Figure 2-53). The reason why we're not using the Edit mode for this example is because it isn't the default mode for the Layout workspace.

Figure 2-53 shows adding materials to some text.

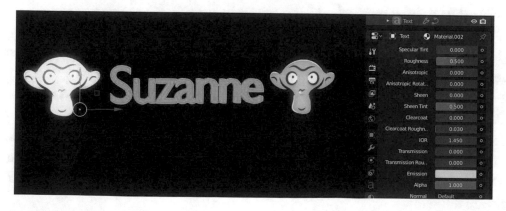

Figure 2-53. *Adding materials to Text*

As you can see, you only use the Emission part of the Principled Shader in the Material mode for the Text. But in this way, you cannot add strength to the emission. There is also a separate Emission Shader, where you can set the strength by clicking the small circle on the surface and choose Emission Shader. Note that you should use the Eevee Render engine here.

Figure 2-54 shows how you can add modifiers to text.

Figure 2-54. *Solidify Modifier for Text object*

Here you add a solidify modifier for text and set its thickness to 0.17m. In the modifier, there is this camera icon and a monitor icon. Camera icon indicates that the effect of a modifier appears in the render mode/rendered image while the monitor icon indicates that the effect appears in the viewport. The up/down arrow arrange modifiers. The arrangement of modifiers affects its output. The X icon deletes the modifier. You can click the Apply button if you are satisfied with the setup of your modifier, and copy to duplicate the modifier selected.

For the area light, add a little green to the default white color and set the watts from 10w to 20w. You should also scale it out to your preferred size, which covers almost part of the stage.

For the Suzanne mesh, you need to first go to Add menu ➤ Mesh ➤ and click Monkey to add it. Or press Shift+A, go to Mesh and click Monkey.

Now add a subsurface modifier for the Suzanne mesh and set its render to 3. The material for it is a little experiment: Base color is Gradient Texture, Subsurface Value is 0.118, Subsurface Color is 4F8CE7, Subsurface radius is 1.000/0.200/0.100, and the others are the same.

For the camera, adjust its location and rotation by using the Local under Transformation Orientation. Make sure it takes the front view of the scene.

Figure 2-55 shows the project in the Layout workspace.

Figure 2-55. *Scene at the Layout workspace*

You can see that the vertical plane has some excess. It's better for you to create an excess because it creates an illusion of continuity in your image rather create something that is fixed on the image size you're creating.

Figure 2-56 shows its final render image.

Figure 2-56. *Final render of Suzanne*

When rendering an image, you can go to Render ➤ Render Image or press F12 then a new window pops up where your image is rendered. To save the image, go to Image ➤ Save As. You could also hold Shift+S, which opens a file browser where you can select the folder to save your image in, as well the image's file extension.

Figure 2-55 shows how I did my lighting. Figure 2-56 shows the overall effect of the lighting.

Lighting

Lighting is one of the critical parts of creating a scene even back then in traditional arts. Colors are affected by how you implement the lighting in your art. Lighting can either help you create an amazing art or destroy your art.

As you can see in my render image, Figure 2-56, my scene isn't dark though it isn't that bright too. I used four objects to light my scene. Area Light is the main one. The three minor ones were the Suzanne grease pencils using Luminance and Glow Effect, and the Suzanne text object using Emission shader. Small changes in this setup affect the scene, as shown in Figure 2-57.

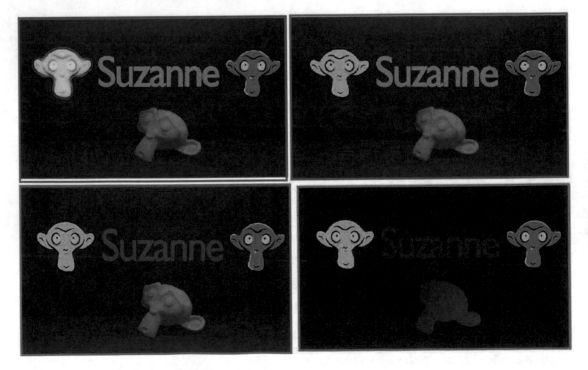

Figure 2-57. *Different renders of Suzzanne*

In the rendered image in the blue rectangle in Figure 2-57, there is an imbalance in the scene after I deleted the Luminance effect in one of the Grease Pencil objects. When you look at the render in the violet rectangle, the Suzanne grease pencils become ordinary.

In the green rectangle, you see how going from Emission Shader to a simple shader affects the text object and the scene. What I did with the three objects didn't directly affect the lighting of the scene, but it did affect the appeal of the scene. Remember, it depends on how you create your lighting. It also creates the mood of your scene.

On the right, you can see the effect when I deleted the main light, which is the area light. It turns dark. It is not completely dark because of the global lighting, which is the lighting set for the entire 3D Viewport. This lighting is the color that you can set in the World category.

In the fourth render, the mesh is almost its silhouette but the Grease Pencil objects and the Text object can still be seen. This is because of the color that I used. I can say that Light and Color are closely related. In what way? There is a saying that the absence of light is black and the presence of light means white. The other colors are created due to interceptions between the two.

Did you ever face your monitor toward sunlight while working and notice differences in color, depending on the angle you are looking at? Though this happens to me by accident it is how light affects the color. It depends on the angle of the light source.

Figure 2-58 shows another example on how lighting works.

Figure 2-58. *Lighting scene at work*

In the scene in Figure 2-58, I used is the **Three-point lighting** technique. Three-point lighting is a method used in visual media such as theatre, video, film, photography and in CGI. By using three light objects in separate positions, you can illuminate a scene however you desire, while controlling the shading and shadows produced by direct lighting.

Three-point lighting is composed of the following. **Key light** shines directly upon the subject and serves as its principal illuminator and more than anything; its strength, color, and angle is the basis of the overall design. **Fill Light** shines on the subject but from the side relative to the position of the Key Light and often positions at a lower place than Key Light. It balances Key Light by illuminating shaded surfaces. Not using a Fill Light at all can result in stark contrast, due to shadows, across the main object's surface. It is usually softer and less bright than the Key light. **Background or Rim Light** shine on the subject from behind, often to one side or the other. It gives the subject a rim of light, serving to separate the subject from the background and highlighting contours. It creates a thin outline around the subject without necessarily hitting the front or visible surface of the subject.

Figure 2-59 shows the difference of these three lights when they act separately.

You can see its difference. When they only act alone, it's not that appealing or the mood is not that bright as what you can see when they are together. That's how much lighting affects your scene.

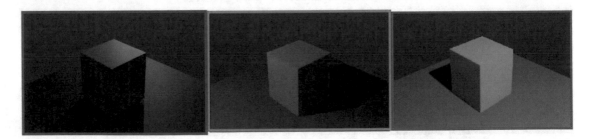

Figure 2-59. *Rim Light (left), Fill Light (middle) and Key Light (right)*

There is another kind of lighting technique called *HDRI images*. It is an easier or quicker way to light your scene. They are essentially snapshots of the real world that contain exquisitely detailed lighting information, which can transport your bland CG objects into realistic virtual environments.

An *HDRI map* is a panoramic photograph that covers the entire field of vision and contains a large amount of data, which emits light into the scene. HDRI stands for High Dynamic Range Image. Dynamic range is the measurement of how much brightness information is contained in an image, so a high dynamic range image is an image that has a very large range of brightness, more than you can see on your screen in one go.

Figure 2-60 shows a sample render with HDRI maps.

Figure 2-60. *HDRI image/map at work, rendered in 2.79 by yours truly*

What you can really do in Layout workspace using Object mode is simple. You can add objects, lighting, and materials. Placing it in desired position and that's it. But there's hope, of course.

CHAPTER 3

Blending with Blender: The Modeling Workspace

This workspace was created for modeling, and you'll learn all about it in this chapter. Again, this chapter starts with a tour of the UI before giving you a sample project to work on. In Figure 3-1, the default mode is Edit mode and Properties are in the Modifier category.

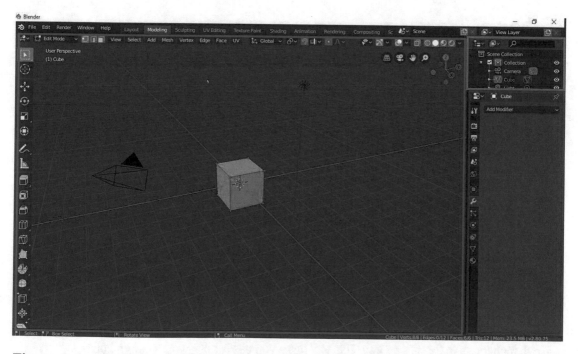

Figure 3-1. *3D Viewport (blue), Outliner (green), and Properties (red)*

In the Modeling workspace, there is the 3D Viewport, Outliner, and Properties. The focus of the discussion is on the Modeling toolbars.

E. T. M. Guevarra, *Modeling and Animation Using Blender*, https://doi.org/10.1007/978-1-4842-5340-3_3

Toolbars

What you can see in a toolbar depends on what type of object are you currently modifying.

I would like to note that objects like Camera, Empty, Force Field, Light, Light Probe, and Speaker don't have an Edit mode. Even if they appear in the Modeling workspace, you can only manipulate their settings when you switch to Object mode.

By default, all toolbars are designed only in one column, but you can make them wider by hovering your mouse at the edge and dragging the black double-sided arrow to the right.

Some of the tools that I discussed in the Layout workspace are also carried out here: the Select tool (arrow icon), the Cursor tool (plus sign inside a circle icon), the Move tool (arrow in four directions), the Rotate tool (two arrows in a circular direction), the Scale tool (small box with small arrow pointing to larger box), the Transform tool (square with four arrows inside a circle), the Annotate tool (pencil icon), and the Measure tool (two rulers).

Since I already discussed these tools in the Layout workspace, I will focus on the tools that are present only when you are in the Modeling workspace or in Edit mode.

CONTEXT MENU

Before we continue to the tools, I'd like to discuss something first. When you click one of the tools using the right mouse button, you see a menu like the one on the left side of Figure 3-2.

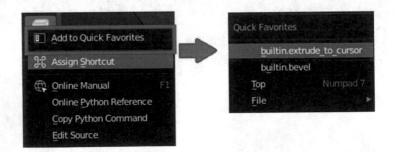

Figure 3-2. *Quick Favorites*

When you click the **Assign Shortcut**, you see a capital **A** pop up. When you hover your mouse in it, it changes to **Press any key**. This tool helps you easily apply your custom hotkeys. Above Assign Shortcut, you see **Add to Quick Favorites**. If you have tools that you often use, you can add it to Quick Favorites for ease of access. To access everything in your Quick Favorites, just press Q on your keyboard, and you see the menu shown on the right side of Figure 3-2. Whatever you add to Quick Favorites appears in that pop-up menu.

Below Assign Shortcut, you see **Online Manual**. Yes, from here, you can look at the documentation about the tool that you are using in Blender to know how it works. When you click that link, you are redirected to the Blender Manual site.

Next is **Online Python Reference**. If you are a developer, you might want to take a look at this one. This one redirects you to the part of the Blender Manual where the source code is documented. This is really for programmers/developers. The Copy Python tool and Edit Source are tools for programmers/developers. If you want to modify a tool, you can use these tools.

Toolbar ➤ Mesh

Figure 3-3 shows the overview of all the tools available in the Modeling workspace toolbar.

Figure 3-3. *Tools in the toolbar for Mesh object*

The leftmost menu in Figure 3-3 is the actual toolbar; what you see on the right side are the tools that appear after you click the small triangle beside the icon. Let's start the discussion.

Since I already discussed many of these tools in the Layout workspace, let's proceed to the tools that are meant for the Mesh object.

Extrude Tool

First, let's discuss the **Extrude tool**, which is used for extruding selected elements. The Extrude tool has four tool types: **Extrude Region (E)**, **Extrude Along Normals (9)**, **Extrude Individual (0)**, and **Extrude to Cursor (Shift+1)**.

Figure 3-4 shows how the Extrude Region tool works.

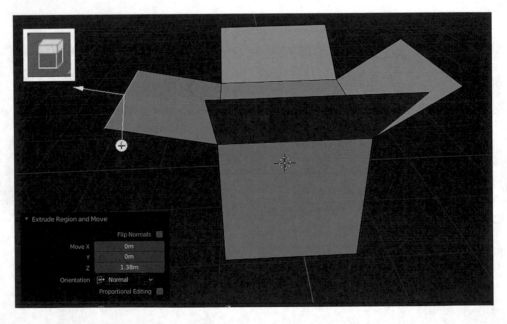

Figure 3-4. *Extrude Region tool and its pop-up menu*

Extrude region means extruding one part of a mesh. There is a plus sign opposite the arrow. When you click it, it changes the direction of where you will extrude. If you want to stop extruding, you can click anywhere else and drag to pull new geometry in that direction. By doing this, a circle appears at the base of the plus to allow further manipulation.

There is another pop-up menu at the bottom of the screen, which is related to the Extrude Region tool. In Figure 3-5, the **Flip Normals** and **Orientation** select menus are visible under the pop-up menu. When you enable the Flip Normals toggle button, you see the arrow with the plus-sign head change its direction to the opposite side. It is different when you click the arrow with the plus-sign head. When you enable/disable flip normals, the arrow with a plus-sign head changes direction to its opposite side without affecting the other arrow. When you click the arrow with the plus-sign head directly, both arrows change direction. Changing the values of x, y, and z affect the length or width of the extruded part.

Orientation is the transformation orientation of your Extrude Region tool. When you enable **Proportional Editing,** settings like Proportional Falloff, Proportional Size, Connected, and Projected (2D) show.

Now, let's proceed to Extrude Along Normals. Figure 3-5 shows how this tool works.

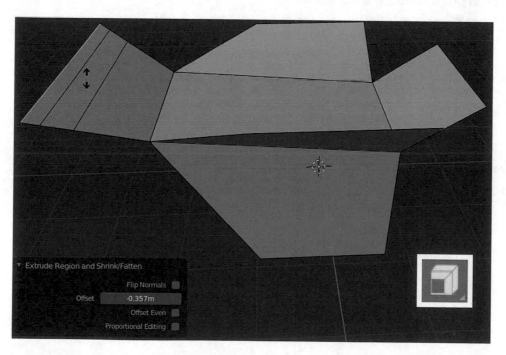

Figure 3-5. *Extrude Along Normals tool*

There is a double-sided black arrow. When using **Extrude Along Normals**, it only extrudes in one direction, which is based on the normal of the element you choose to extrude. In Figure 3-5, I extruded the edge facing in the left side. When I enabled **Flip Normals**, the normals switched direction but not the object. That meant the extruded part went in the opposite direction, which was the right side.

Adjusting the size of the offset adjusts the size of the extruded part. There is proportional editing for this, and the settings are the same as Extrude Region.

Extrude Individual Tool

When you use **Extrude Individual** on vertices and edges, it either moves or scales the elements.

With this tool, when you select a face, it creates other faces to surround it, like a box. In Figure 3-6, the selected face is the one on the left. When I extrude it, it creates other faces in its surroundings.

The icon represents Extrude Individual. It can only extrude faces, as shown in Figure 3-6. Extrude Individual has its own pop-up menu, in which you can set its offset, and it has proportional editing settings.

Figure 3-6 shows how this tool works.

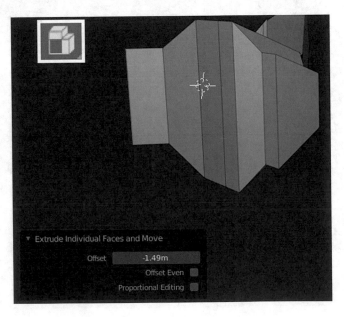

Figure 3-6. *Extrude Individual tool*

Extrude to Cursor Tool

Let's now discuss the **Extrude to Cursor tool (Shift+1)**. Figure 3-7 shows how it works.

Figure 3-7. Extrude to Cursor tool

This method of extruding means to extrude in the direction in which the mouse cursor is located.

Extrude to Cursor has a toggle box for flipping normals, settings to adjust the x, y, and z axes, and settings for orientation and proportional editing. With this method, I advise that you think before you click because this is the direction in which the extruding happens. But if you accidentally click the mouse, you can undo it.

Inset Tool

The purpose of the Inset tool is to insert new faces in the selected faces, as shown in Figure 3-8. When you adjust thickness in the settings, the inset faces adjust their scope; it depends on the measurement or value given. When you adjust a value in the depth settings, the inset face moves either inward or outward, depending on the value. When you enable **Outset**, it outsets instead of insets, which means rather than inward, things move outward when inserting new faces. When you enable **Select Outer**, it selects the new inset faces.

Figure 3-8 shows how it works.

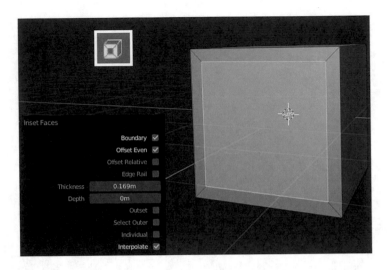

Figure 3-8. *Inset tool*

When you enable **Individual**, it insets the face individually. When you enable **Interpolate**, it blends the face data across the inset. **Boundary** insets face boundaries. **Offset Even** scales the offset to even the thickness. **Offset Relative** scales the offset of the surrounding geometry. **Edge Rail** insets the region along existing edges. By default, Boundary, Offset Even, and Interpolate are enabled because the combination of the three is enough to offer a nice inset for basic or simple designs.

Bevel Tool

Next, is the **Bevel tool (Ctrl+B)**. Figure 3-9 shows how this tool works.

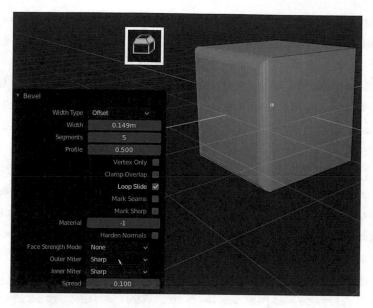

Figure 3-9. *Bevel tool*

The Bevel is the tool that is most used, especially by those who make photorealistic scenes. In reality, there is no perfect cube, rectangle, or any other shape; that's why there is the Bevel tool. This tool smooths the edges of a mesh; the amount depends on the settings you make. By default, the segment value is 0, but as you can see in Figure 3-9, the segment value is 5, which makes the edges smoother because it creates five loops around that edges or segments.

The **Width** value is the scope of the bevel. There are four types: Offset, Width, Depth, and Percent. By default, the Width type is offset.

When you adjust the value of **Profile**, it changes the way the bevel looks.

When you enable **Vertex Only**, the bevel is applicable only on the corners, vertices mesh, or edges that are currently selected.

Clamp Overlap prevents the beveled edges or vertices from overlapping.

When **Loop Slide** is activated, it slides the unbeveled edges along with beveled edges into a vertex. Turning it off can lead to even widths.

Mark Seams is used if you want to mark seams along the beveled edges. Seams are a way to create separations, which are useful for UV mapping.

Mark Sharp marks the beveled edges as sharp. Sharp is used by the edge split modifier, which is a smoothing technique.

Material is the shader or material used in the beveled edges. The material currently selected in the Material panel under the Properties Editor will reflect as the material for the beveled edges. The default number is –1. The material is inherited from the closest existing face; otherwise, the number is the slot index of the material to use for all newly created faces.

When **Hardened Normals** is enabled, the per-vertex face normals of the bevel face are adjusted to match the surrounding faces, and the normals of the surrounding faces are not affected. This keeps the surrounding faces flat, and with the bevel faces smoothly shading into them.

Face Strength Mode is to set strength face in the faces involved in the bevel mode. There are four options: None, All, Affected, and New. By default, this is set to None.

There is also **Outer Miter** and **Inner Miter**. First, what is a miter? A miter is formed when two beveled objects meet at an angle. Outer Miter has three options: Patch, Sharp, and Arc. Inner Miter has two options: Sharp and Arc. When you choose Patch, the edges meet at a sharp point. Two extra vertices are introduced near the point so that the edges and faces at the vertex are less pinched together. When you choose Sharp, the edges meet at a sharp point with no extra vertices introduced on the edges. When you choose Arc, two vertices are introduced near the meeting point, and a curved arc joins them together.

Loop Cut and Offset Edge Loop Cut Tools

The next tools are **Loop Cut** (Ctrl+R) and **Offset Edge Loop Cut** (Shift+Ctrl+R).

You can set the number of loop cuts in the pop-up menu for the Loop Cut tool. Adjusting the **Smoothness** value in the settings makes the loop cut go inward or outward. **Falloff** is about the smoothness type, and it changes the shape of the profile. Falloff has six types: Linear, Sharp, Inverse Square, Root, Sphere, and Smooth. **Factor** adjusts the place of the active loop cuts. Enabling **Even** makes the edge loop match the shape of the adjacent edge loop. **Flipped** flips the target edge loop to match when **Even** is enabled.

Offset Edge Loop Cut adds two edge loops on either side of the selected loops, while Loop Cut inserts a new loop intersecting the chosen edge. It has the same settings as Loop Cut except that it does have Cap Endpoint and it doesn't have Falloff. When you enable Cap Endpoint, it extends the loop around the endpoints.

Figure 3-10 shows how the Loop Cut tool works.

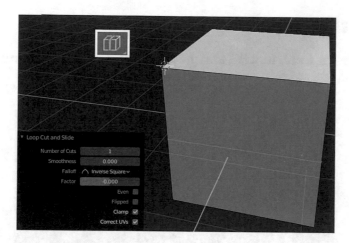

Figure 3-10. *Loop Cut tool at work*

Figure 3-11 shows the Offset Edge Loop Cut tool.

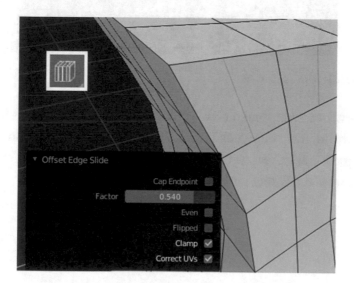

Figure 3-11. *Offset Edge Loop Cut tool*

Note   If you emulate the numpad, the hotkeys using 0–9 on your keyboard will not work because they are replaced by the numpad tools. For example, 4 is a hotkey for Annotate, but if you are emulating the numpad, it turns into a hotkey for Orbit Left, which originally had a Numpad 4 hotkey. We discuss a lot of hotkeys, but I'd like you to remember this one.

Knife and Bisect Tools

The next tools are the **Knife tool** (K) and the **Bisect tool** (Shift+2). Figure 3-12 shows how the Knife tool works.

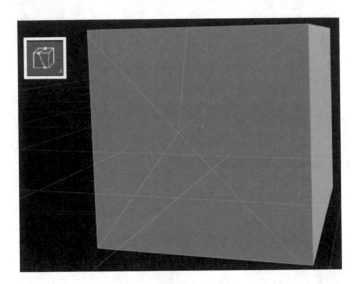

Figure 3-12. *Knife tool at work*

Knife, unlike other tools, doesn't have many settings. It does things like an actual knife in the real world. It cuts the meshes according to the direction you want and creates new vertices; it ends when you hit Enter.

Figure 3-13 shows the Bisect tool.

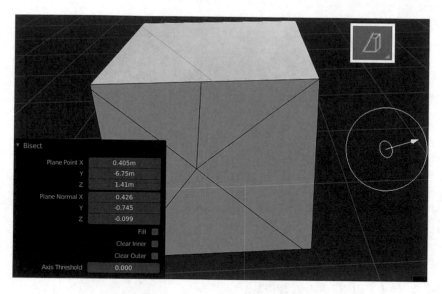

Figure 3-13. *Bisect tool at work*

Knife only works in selected faces, but the **Bisect** tool works on the whole mesh.

As you can see, there is a circle with an arrow inside near a mesh when you used a Bisect tool. This arrow is the basis of the tool's direction or the axis it will start bisecting.

In the pop-up menu settings, there is **Plane Point**. When you adjust the value of the x, y, or z axes in Plane Point, you see the arrow and the loop in the Bisect tool move at the same time. Plane Point sets the point in the plane, which is the loop created by the Bisect tool.

Plane Normal is the direction of the plane point. By default, the Bisect tool only divides the existing face, but when you enable **Fill**, it fills the cut portion of the mesh. Enabling fill connects the vertices created by the Bisect tool, and forms another face. When you enable **Clear Inner**, it cuts out the geometry behind the plane. **Clear Outer** cuts out the geometry in front of the plane.

Polybuild Tool

Let's move on to the **Polybuild tool** (Shift+3). Figure 3-14 shows how this tool works.

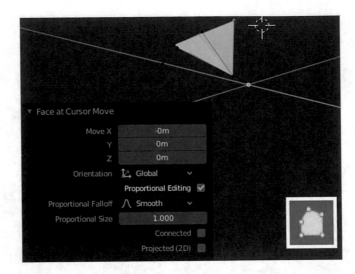

Figure 3-14. *Polybuild tool at work*

To use this tool, you need to create a shape from the vertices.

The Polybuild tool is a way to start a mesh. It is more useful when doing retopology. For you to use it, first, create three or four vertices using this tool and then create a face by clicking the F key. When you hover on the edge or in the vertex, it turns pink. Try to drag it using your left mouse button, and you will create another plane. That's how the Polybuild tool works. Simple, isn't it?

Spin and Spin Duplicates Tool

Let's proceed to the next tools, which are the **Spin** tool (Shift+4) and the **Spin Duplicates** tool (Shift+5). Figure 3-15 shows how the Spin tool works.

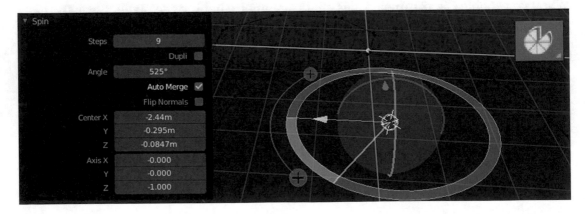

Figure 3-15. *Spin tool at work*

To use the Spin tool, you must have an existing vertex or vertices that it can extrude. It extrudes in a circular direction. The Spin tool settings are quite simple. **Steps** indicate the number of vertices to be added in the current vertices in the scene.

The rest of the settings are for rotating, scaling, or moving the mesh in the x, y, or z axes. There is a guide that helps you with this. Figure 3-15 shows the guide for working with the Spin tool. When you hold and drag the blue curve with the plus icon in its head, it creates vertices around it while spinning. When you drag one of the two arrows, the created vertices rotate toward the axis, represented by the arrow you dragged. It's best to play around with this tool. You might create something amazing from it.

Spin Duplicates is the same as the Spin tool, except that it duplicates the data of the object or the elements.

Smooth Tool

The **Smooth** tool (Shift+6) flattens angles of the selected vertices. The **Randomize** tool (Shift+7) randomly arranges selected vertices.

Edge Slide and Vertex Slide Tool

The **Edge Slide** tool (Shift+8) and the **Vertex Slide** (Shift+V) have the same function and settings. The only difference is the way that they affect the element. Figure 3-16 shows how the Edge Slide and Vertex Slide tools work.

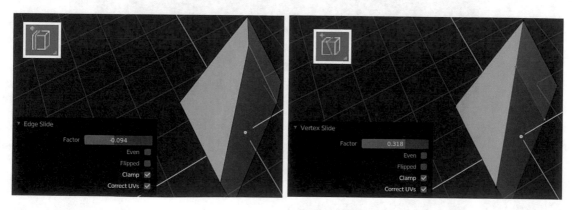

Figure 3-16. *Edge slide at work (left) and vertex slide at work (right)*

The settings for **Factor** are for the distance of the element. Enabling **Even** makes the edge loop match the shape of the adjacent edge loop. Enabling **Flipped** makes an edge loop flip between the two adjacent loops when Even is enabled. Enabling **Clamp** makes an edge clamp within the edge extents. Enabling **Correct UVs** automatically corrects UV coordinates while transforming.

Shrink/Flatten Tool

The Shrink/Flatten tool (Alt+S) is like a scale tool when you use it in an ordinary mesh, except that it has settings, like proportional editing.

The offset, proportional editing, falloff, and other settings function the same as I discussed in previous tools. What I discuss here is how you visually see the effects of this tool. This tool shrinks and flattens the vertices along normals. For trial purposes, to see its effect, we must first select parts of the mesh.

To feel the effects of proportional editing, you need a lot of vertices.

Figure 3-17 shows how the Shrink/Flatten tool works.

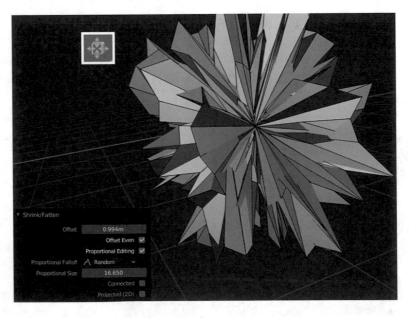

Figure 3-17. *Shrink/Flatten tool at work*

It is more interesting with proportional editing. It should be noted that once you go to the Adjustment panel to enable proportional editing, you can't click out of the panel. When you play around with the offset and match it with the right proportional editing falloff and size, you can create something amusing.

Push/Pull Tool

The Push/Pull tool (Shift+9) pushes or pulls selected items or elements. Figure 3-18 shows the tool's settings and how it works.

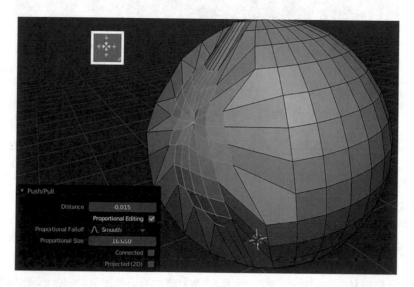

Figure 3-18. *Push/Pull tool at work*

This tool has the same settings as the Shrink/Flatten tool except that the Push/Pull tool works directly on the selected element.

Shear Tool

Now, let's move on to the next tool, which is the **Shear** tool (Shift+Ctrl+Alt+S). The Shear tool shears selected items along the horizontal axis of the screen.

When you select the Shear tool, there are arrows pointing to different axes appearing on the selected elements to modify. When you click and drag the head of this arrow, which is looks like the letter X, the selected element is sheared to the x axis, of toward the y axis, or even in the z axis; it depends on which direction the X line is pointing to. You can also change the direction by changing the offset value and changing the axis in the Settings panel.

Figure 3-19 shows how the Shear tool works.

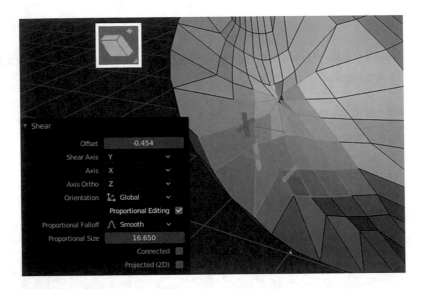

Figure 3-19. *Shear tool at work*

To Sphere Tool

The **To Sphere** tool (Shift+Alt+S) simply moves the vertices in a spherical shape when you create a new face or a new part of the mesh.

Just like in the Shrink/Flatten and Push/Pull tools, the right amount of factor, proportional falloff, and size can give you an amazing outcome. Just explore, experiment, and play. That's how creativity works!

Before we proceed to the last tool in the Modeling workspace, I'd like you to look at Figure 3-20. It shows the products of a few experiments using the Shrink/Flatten, Push/Pull, Shear, and To Sphere tools.

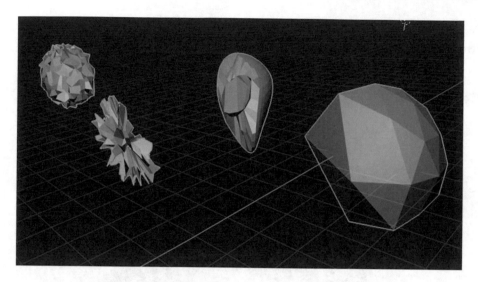

Figure 3-20. *Experiments using Shrink/Flatten, Push/Pull, Shear, To Sphere tools*

Rip Region and Rip Edge Tools

Let's proceed to the last tools, which are **Rip Region** (V) and **Rip Edge** (Alt+D). Rip Region rips polygons and moves the result. Rip Edge rips the vertices and moves the result. Figure 3-21 shows how Rip Region and Rid Edge work.

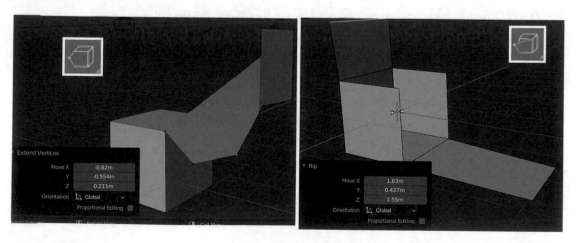

Figure 3-21. *Rip Region (left) and Rip Edge (right)*

As you can see in Figure 3-21, **Rip Region** extends the vertices and automatically connects them to other vertices. **Rip Edge** extends the edge and cuts or rips it out from the mesh. These tools can only be used with the vertices and the edge.

We're done with Mesh tools. We'll proceed to the tools for the Armature object. I will only briefly discuss these tools since they are advanced.

Toolbar ➤ Armature

Figure 3-22 shows what's inside the Armature toolbar.

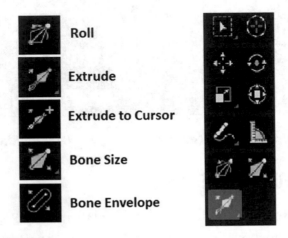

Figure 3-22. *Specific tools (left) and Armature toolbar (right)*

Roll (Ctrl+Alt+S) transforms selected items by rotating or rolling.

Bone Size (9) and **Bone Envelope** (0) transform selected items by mode type. The difference between the two is that Bone Envelope indirectly affects a bone, while Bone Size directly affects a bone.

Extrude (E) creates new bones from the selected joints and moves them.

Extrude to Cursor (Shift+1) extrudes the bones where you click your cursor. (Think before you click.)

Let's move on to the set of tools for the Grease Pencil object.

Toolbar ➤ Grease Pencil

Figure 3-23 shows what's inside the Grease Pencil toolbar.

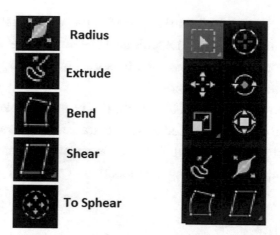

Figure 3-23. Specific tools (left) and Grease Pencil toolbar (right)

Radius (Alt+S) contracts or expands the radius of the selected points.

Extrude (5) creates another stroke from the selected points.

Bend (Shift+W) bends selected items between the 3D cursor and the mouse.

Shear (Shift+Ctrl+Alt+S) shears selected items along the horizontal screen axis.

To Sphere (Shift+Alt+S) moves selected vertices outward in a spherical shape around the mesh center.

Let's proceed to the set of tools for Curve objects.

Toolbar ➤ Curve

Figure 3-24 shows the list of tools for the Curve object.

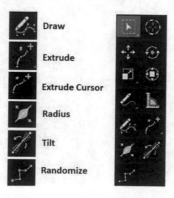

Figure 3-24. Specific tools (left) and Curve toolbar (right)

Since what we have for Surface, Lattice and Metaball are only the Select tools, Cursor, Rotate, Scale tools, Transform, Annotate tools and Measure while on Text Objects, what we have are only Cursor, Annotate tools and Measure, I will not explain it since I already discuss those tools in the previous topics.

The Camera, Empty, Force Field, Light, Light Probe, and Speaker objects don't have an Edit mode; they can only be modified by simple transformations in Object mode. Therefore, they are not part of the Modeling workspace discussion.

Let's work on a simple project using the tools.

Sample Project

Let's edit our Suzanne project using a combination of the Layout workspace (or Object mode) and the Modeling workspace (or Edit mode). Remember, Object mode is the default mode for the Layout workspace, and Edit mode is the default mode for the Modeling workspace.

Figure 3-25 shows the current setup of Suzanne's project.

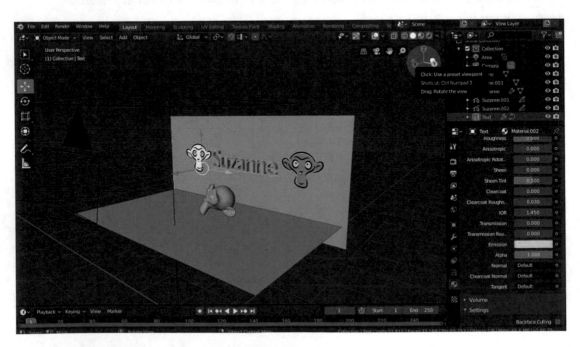

Figure 3-25. *The current setup for Project Suzanne*

Figure 3-26 shows how we'll use the Extrude Region and Bevel tools in this project.

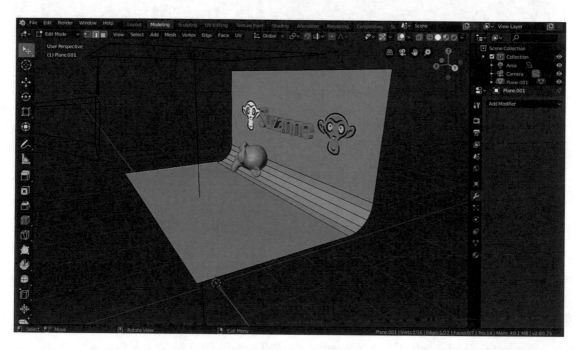

Figure 3-26. *The Extrude Region and Bevel tools at work on Project Suzanne*

First, delete one of the planes and re-create it in the Modeling workspace using the Extrude Region tool. Next, switch from vertex to edge before using the tool. You should choose the bottom edge and extrude it. Then select the edge in the center (the edge that separates the two planes) using the Select tool. Finally, use the Bevel tool and set the segment value to 5.

Now you'll use the Mirror Modifier. Figure 3-27 shows an example in Edit mode. To do this, hide a grease pencil and select the other one. Then go to Edit mode and press A (to select all) and move the object toward the right side. Go back to Object mode, select the object, and add Mirror Modifier. Make sure that the Xin the modifier setting is checked because it means mirrored in the x axis.

Figure 3-27. *Mirror modifier in Edit mode*

Now go to Edit mode. Go to the grease pencil object data in Properties, where you see the Layers panel contains Fill and Strokes. In this panel, you can choose to disable viewing the fill or the strokes in the viewport. Choose to disable viewing the strokes for this project because you will separately apply the materials to the Suzanne grease pencil. As you can see in Figure 3-28, it was already treated as an object. Therefore, when you apply materials, this applies to both of them.

Figure 3-28. *Mirror modifier in Object mode*

In Figure 3-29, the Materials section in Edit mode creates two colors for the skin. This is to assign different colors to the two grease pencils.

Compared to the Layout workspace or Object mode, the Materials setting in Edit mode (or the Modeling workspace) has a lot of options. Choose a part of your object, click the material in the panel, and then click the Assign button to apply the material. To add new materials from the list for the same object, you just need to click the **plus button**. To delete existing materials, click the **minus button**.

Figure 3-29 shows a close-up.

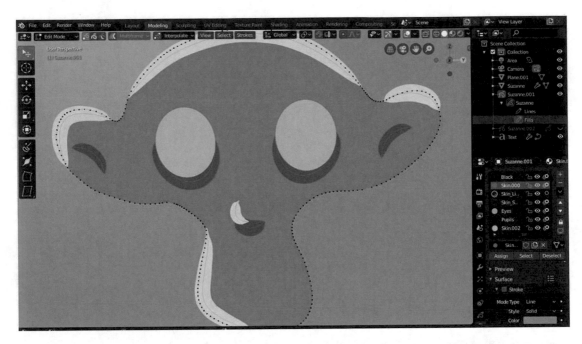

Figure 3-29. *Selecting the part of Grease pencil and assigning material*

Figure 3-30 shows the final result of this technique.

Figure 3-30. *Result of the technique*

As you can see in Figure 3-30 and Figure 3-31, although this method might be time-consuming and very detailed, you will be happy with the result.

For final modifications, let's add hair particles to the mesh Suzanne object using the Particles setting in Properties.

1. Click the Add button. Set Hair Length to 0.02m and the number value to 20,000.

2. Set Strand Shape to 1, Radius Root to 1.1m, Tip to 0.11m, and Radius Scale to 0.02. There are all settings under Hair Shape.

3. Click Advanced to enable the Rotation setting. Set Randomize to 0.123.

4. Switch from Edit mode to Particle Edit in Mode Type.

Figure 3-31 shows what you have accomplished.

Figure 3-31. *Result of the technique, part 2*

Make sure that your normal (or the lines sticking out from your mesh object) is facing upward or outside the mesh. Go to Edit mode ➤ Mesh ➤ Normals ➤ Flip Normals.

I'd like to note that once you enter Particle Edit mode and start to edit your particle, you can no longer change your settings in Properties, unless you delete your edits by clicking the **Delete Edit** button.

Now use **Cut** (8) in the toolbar to cut the hair from Suzanne's mouth and eyes. You should also use the **Comb tool** (3) to comb the hair, and then the **Puff tool** (7) to make more adjustments. You can add hair using the **Add tool** (5). Finally, use the **Smooth tool** (4) to get the desired order of the hair particles.

After you're satisfied with the hair particles, add materials by using the Edit mode settings for it. You will only apply simple materials here because I have not yet explained the Shading workspace, where you can do more experiments in the Materials settings.

Figure 3-32 shows the output.

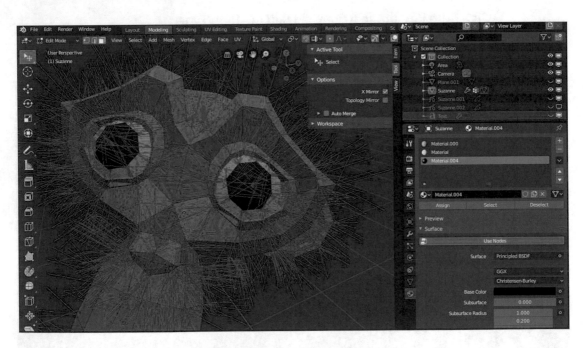

Figure 3-32. *Result of the technique, part 3*

The last stage is to adjust the Area light. Change the color a little and adjust the watts to 30. Next, add a subsurface modifier to the plane and add two or three loop cuts to maintain the edges, because when you apply a subsurface modifier in an object, it smoothens the edges of the object to make it look like a circle.

Figure 3-33 shows the final rendered image.

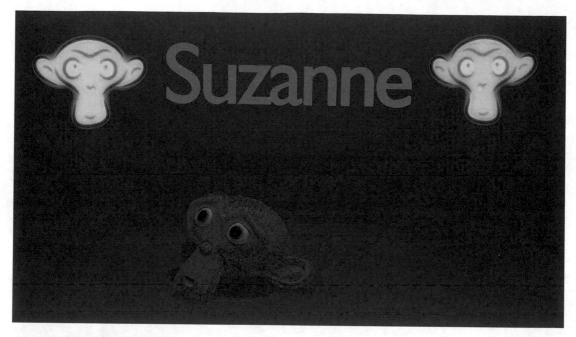

Figure 3-33. *Final render*

Still simple? Yes.

We have lots of tools in Blender, like the **Particle Edit Mode**, which can help you to create awesome scenes.

Let's proceed to the last workspace. Chapter 4 covers the Shading workspace.

CHAPTER 4

Blending with Blender: The Shading Workspace

We're now in the workspace that can help you create awesome materials. This chapter contains the usual tour, followed by a sample project, and then some cool samples by other Blender artists. Let's start the tour with Figure 4-1, which shows the workspace.

Figure 4-1. *File Browser (blue), 3D Viewport (red), Image Editor (violet), Shader Editor (green), Outliner (orange) and Properties (yellow)*

© Ezra Thess Mendoza Guevarra 2020
E. T. M. Guevarra, *Modeling and Animation Using Blender*, https://doi.org/10.1007/978-1-4842-5340-3_4

The Shader workspace is composed of six parts. The **File Browser** is in the top left of the workspace. The **3D Viewport** is in LookDev Shading mode and located in the top center of the workspace. **Outliner** is located in the top right of the workspace. The **Image Editor** is located at the bottom left of the workspace. The **Shader Editor** is located at the bottom center of the workspace. **Properties** is located on the right side of the workspace.

You already know about Properties, Outliner, and 3D Viewport. Let's discuss the File Browser, Image Editor, and Shader Editor.

File Browser

File browser is a common term in the computer world. You cannot explore your files without it. It's the same in Blender. File Browser allows you to open your files—.blend files, textures, images, downloaded objects, or anything that you need to complete your project or scene.

Figure 4-2 shows the File Browser.

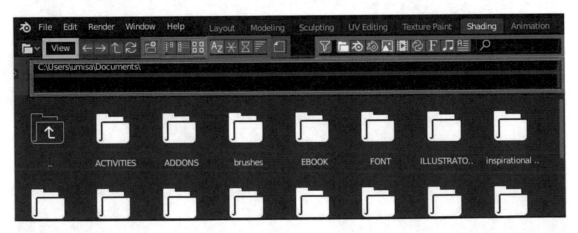

Figure 4-2. *File Browser: View (pink), Navigation (red), Create New Directory (green), Display Mode (brown), File Sorting (violet), Show Hidden Files (blue), File Filtering (light blue), File Path (yellow)*

In Figure 4-2, you can see the common tools in File Browser. If you are currently in front of Blender 2.80, you already know where these tools are in File Browser, and I don't need to discuss it much.

- **View** has three submenus. **Display Size** is the size of the column in your file browser. **Recursion** is the level of searching. **Area** is the display screen.

- **Navigation** is used for browsing folders.

- **Create New Directory** helps you create a new folder directly from Blender when you want your file to be in a specific folder that isn't available in the current path.

- **Display Mode** helps you see the file in a view that is comfortable for you. It can be in thumbnail view, short-list view, or long-list view.

- **File Sorting** and **File Filtering** help you easily find files. There are a lot of files and file types inside a folder. You can filter (e.g., make them all .blend files and list them alphabetically) to let you easily find what you're looking for.

- **Show Hidden Files** opens a hidden file. If it happens that any media or project that you use here is hidden, you made it hidden for some purpose.

- **File Path** is where you can see the path of your file, as shown in Figure 4-2, or directly open your project. The folder with an arrow is for browsing your files.

Now, let's move on to the Image Editor.

Image Editor

The **Image Editor** is where you can view and edit 2D assets, such as images or textures. You can see in Figure 4-3 that it has a header, a toolbar, a sidebar, and a big square with a grid. Image Editor is a multilayered editor, which means that when a rendered image is displayed in this editor, several new menu items become available.

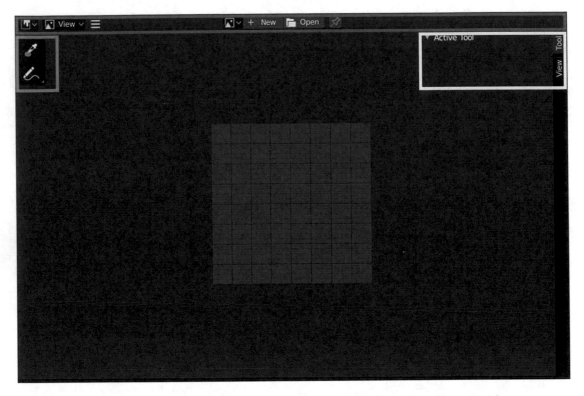

Figure 4-3. *Image Editor header (top), sidebar (right) and toolbar (left)*

By default, the toolbar (T) and the sidebar (N) are hidden. The big square at the center with grids in it is called **Slot.** This is where you see the image that you want to edit. You can save successive renders into the render buffer by selecting a new slot before rendering. If an image has been rendered to a slot, it can be viewed by selecting that slot.

In **Header**, there is View, New, and Open. This View Select menu has three different modes that you can choose in editing your image: View, Paint, and Mask.

In the Sidebar region, there is the Tools panel, where you can see your active tool, and the View panel, where you can have annotations.

This is the setup when there is no image in Image Editor. Figure 4-4 shows what happens when we open an image here.

Figure 4-4. *Image Editor upon opening an image*

As you can see in Figure 4-4, after we open an image, there are changes in the Header region as well as in the Sidebar region. There are four additional icons in the Header region; while in the Sidebar region, there are two additional panels.

I'd like to note that there are differences in the tool/command terms in the Image Editor (shown in the Shading workspace) and the Image Editor (shown in the Rendering workspace, which is covered in Chapter 5).

So, let's discuss the Image Editor tools for the Shading workspace.

Tools

The shield icon in the Header region is called **Fake User**. It saves the current data-block, even it has no user; for example, the image we currently opened. Even it isn't used as a material, it is saved for future use.

The icon next to it is **New Image,** which creates a new image. The folder icon is **Open**, which opens an image.

The X icon is **Delete**, which unlinks a data-block or the image. When you click it, the image disappears; you see again in the default Image Editor setup. If you accidentally delete something and want to bring it back without browsing the file once again, you need to click the image icon next to the File Search box, and there you can see the list of the images opened in the Image Editor. I'd like to note that even you use annotations here, when you delete the image, what you drew using the annotation remains. When you bring back an image after having changed its values in the Scope panel, the value is not reset.

In the toolbar, there is **Sample,** which picks sample pixel values under the cursor. The list of Annotate tools is always present: Annotate (2), Annotate Line (3), Annotate Polygon (4), and Annotate Eraser (5).

Now, let's discuss the Sidebar region.

Sidebar

There are panels for tools, images, views, and scopes.

Tool Panel

The **Tool panel** features the settings for the active tool or the tool you're currently using. Since Image Editor only has five tools, its settings aren't complicated. The **Draw tool** allows you to see settings for the radius. It is the same for Annotate Eraser, but for Annotate, Annotate Line, and Annotate Polygon, what you can see in its setting are color and notes.

Figure 4-5 shows the Tool panel.

Figure 4-5. *Image Editor ➤ Tool panel with Annotation*

Image Panel

The **Image** panel's settings contain the **Source**, which indicates where the image came from. The settings that follow depend on the options you choose in the source. There are four options available: Single, Image Sequence, Movie, and Generated.

If you choose **Single Image,** the settings available include a box in which you can see the file name and the exact location of your image.

Pack Image, sitting at the left side of file name, packs an image as an embedded data in the blend file.

The **Open/Accept** button, the folder icon beside the file name, opens or browses the image in the file directory.

The **Reload Image** (Alt+R) button beside the Open/Accept button, reloads the current image from the disk.

Color Space indicates the color space in the image file to convert to and from when saving and loading the image. There are seven options: sRGB, Filmic Log, Linear, Linear ACES, Non-Color, Raw, and XYZ.

Alpha is the representation of alpha in the image file. There are four options: Straight, Premultiplied, Channel Packed, and None.

View as Render renders part of the display transformation.

Meta Data is the code data of the image.

Figure 4-6 shows the effects of color space on an image.

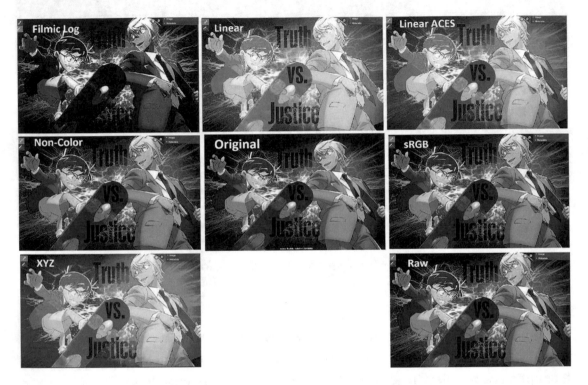

Figure 4-6. *Color Space on image*

The original image shown in Figure 4-6 is not yet imported in Blender 3D. As you can see, Non-Color, Raw, sRGB, and the original, which is in RGB, do not seem to have any differences, unlike what you can see in Filmic Log, Linear, Linear ACES, and XYZ.

First, what is **Color Space**? Once upon a time, human met the machine. Human wanted to create art with the machine but the machine couldn't understand human language. One day, human found a way to break this boundary. Since machine could understand numbers and human was a genius in math, they created a number to represent each color. Red = 0%, Green = 0%, Blue = 0% means Black. Red = 100%, Green = 100%, Blue = 100% means White. Red = 100%, Green = 100%, Blue = 0% means Yellow. This is called *color space*. In other words, color space is the mathematical expression of color for the machine to understand it.

sRGB, Non-Color, Raw, Filmic Log, Linear, Linear ACES, and XYZ are the mapping of colors, created for digital purposes. To have a standard way of dealing with colors, sRGB was created by Microsoft and HP and is said to be the standard way of communicating with colors in many digital forms.

So now, let's go back to the Image panel settings for Image Editor.

When you are in Filmic Log, Linear, Linear ACES, or sRGB, the Alpha setting is enabled, but when you are in Non-Color and Raw, it is disabled.

When the Source is set to **Image Sequence**, the setting is the same in Single Image. In **Image Sequence**, **Frames** indicates the number of images to use in a movie. *Start*, sets the global starting frame of the movie or sequence, assuming the first picture is numbered 1. **Offset** offsets the number frames in the animation. Cyclic cycles the images in the movie. **Auto Refresh**, which is enabled by default, refreshes an image on frame changes.

Image Sequence is used in animation and movie clips. In Source, the **Movie** option has the same settings as Image Sequence but includes **Deinterlace**, which deinterlaces a movie file on load.

Figure 4-7 shows Source**'s Generated** settings.

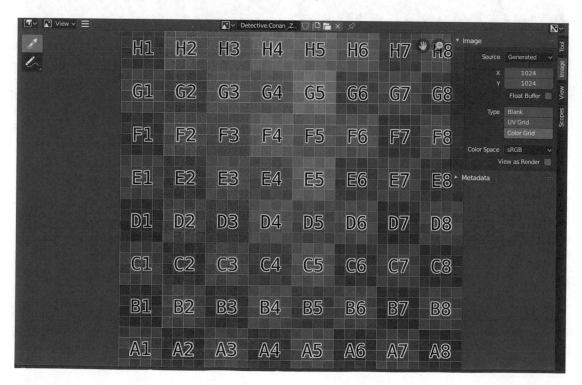

Figure 4-7. *Image panel when Source is in Generated*

What happened to the two anime characters? When the source is in Generated, it converts the image into blocks of color. Its settings are quite different, as you can see in Figure 4-7. It has **X/Y**, which indicates the generated size of an image. **Float Buffer** generates a floating-point buffer. **Type** allows you to choose the generated image type. **Blank** leaves the slot blank. **UV Grid** makes it looks like a colored plus sign in a line in the slot. **Color Grid** is shown in Figure 4-7. It also offers Color Space and View in Render, which is enabled by default.

I'd like to note that when you select Generated and you go back to Single Image, you will not see your image in the slot—even if it is opened in the Header region. If you open it from the image list, you will not see it. In the settings, there is a notification that it can't load the image, which is because Generated generates another image from the current opened image. It replaces it in the saved list in the Blender cache but it does not replace the file in your disk. If you want to use the original file, the best solution is to reopen the image with the **Open/Accept** button.

Now, let's proceed to the Image Editor **View** panel.

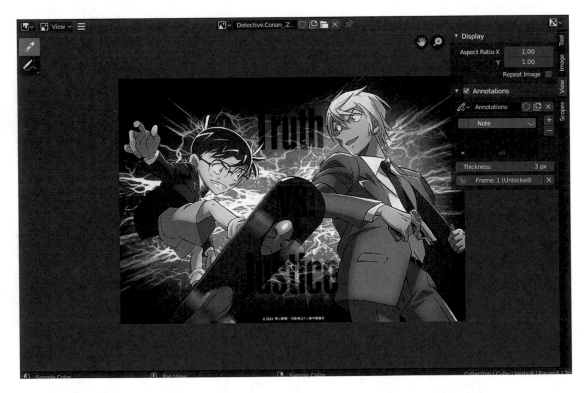

Figure 4-8. *View panel*

As you can see in Figure 4-8, the View panel's settings are simple, just like the Tool panel. The **Aspect Ratio X/Y** displays the aspect. **Repeat Image** displays the image repeatedly outside of the main view. **Annotation** allows you to see the color of the note, the thickness of the annotate tool, and to delete and add notes.

The **Scope** panel has five setting: Histogram, Waveform, Vectorscope, Sample Line, and Sample.

In **Histogram**, you see the graphical expression of the color data in your image, as shown in Figure 4-9. It has Luma channel, RGB channel, Red Channel, Green channel, Blue channel, and Alpha channel. The button on the left is **Show Line**, which shows lines instead of filled shapes when showing the data in the histogram.

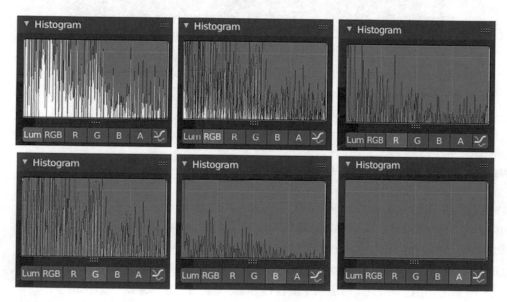

Figure 4-9. *Scope panel ➤ Histogram*

Figure 4-9 shows that there is a lot of green in my image but little blue. A luma represents the brightness in an image.

Now, let's proceed to **Waveform**, as shown in Figure 4-10.

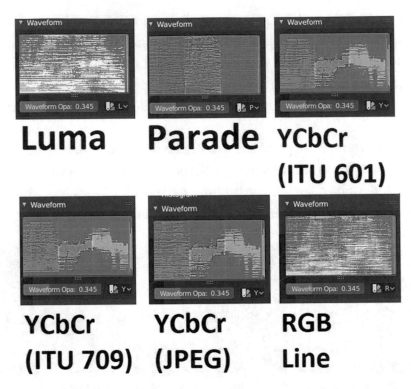

Figure 4-10. *Scope panel ➤ Waveform*

Just like in the Histogram, you can see the color data of an image by category. Waveform displays luminance with IRE values. IRE represents the scale invented by the International Radio Engineers Society. Essentially, it is designed to match the capabilities of early televisions to display an image. Anything at 0 is completely black, with no detail, and anything above 100 is clipped and white, with no detail.

Now, let's proceed to **Vectorscope** (see Figure 4-11).

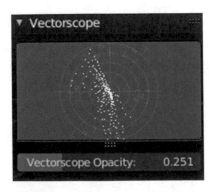

Figure 4-11. *Scope panel ➤ Vectorscope*

Vectorscope shows the hue and saturation. It displays six color targets fixed into an odd-shaped pattern on a grid. In fact, each color is represented by two targets; but what is important about the vectorscope is that it displays color information that the waveform monitor does not.

Now, let's proceed to **Sample Line** and **Samples.** Figure 4-12 shows its settings.

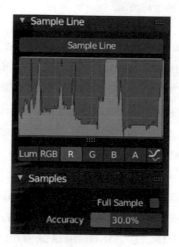

Figure 4-12. *Scope panel ➤ Vectorscope*

These two settings get a color data sample from a particular part of an image. When you click the sample line, it creates a line for you to select the part of the image to determine the luma content in it. **Full Sample** samples every pixel of the image. **Accuracy** sets the proportion of the original image's source pixel lines to the sample.

Learning scopes can help you get the right balance of color for your project, that's why it is important. We cannot see easily see its effect since it comes with the right combination of adjustments.

This is the end of the discussion on Image Editor. Let's now proceed to the Shader Editor.

Shader Editor

The Shader Editor is where you can create amazing materials using the combination of different nodes. You can also edit materials that are used in Cycles and the Eevee render engine. Materials, lights, and backgrounds are all defined using a network of shading nodes. These nodes output values, vectors, colors, and shaders.

This editor is composed of a header region, a toolbar (T), a sidebar (N), and a node editor.

Header

Figure 4-13 shows the Shader Editor's Header region.

Figure 4-13. *Shader Editor* ➤ *Header*

On the left side, there is the Select menu for the **Editor Type** and the **Shade Type**. The **View menu** consists of commands for viewing the toolbar and sidebar, zooming in/out, viewing selected/all, and different options in the view area. The **Select** menu consists of various commands for selecting things. The **Add** menu adds nodes, which you can do by holding Shift+A in the Node Editor section. The **Node** menu consists of commands for working with nodes.

Use Nodes enables the shader nodes to render the material. **Slot** selects active material for your project. You can also see the materials you already created for a specific object. There are the **Fake User**, **New Material**, and **Delete** buttons. The **Pin Button** keeps the current material selection fixed. There is also an arrow icon at the right side of the Header region pointing upward. This is the **Parent Node Tree**, which is used to go to the parent node tree. It is useful when you already have a lot of nodes, and you group and link node groups. The **Snap Node Element** consists of four options: Grid, Node X, Node Y, and Node X/Y.

Toolbar

Now, let's proceed to the toolbar. If you press T, the toolbar will appear. It consists of the **Select** tool (W) for single selection, **Box Select** (B) for box selection, **Circle Select** (C) for circle selection, the **Lasso** tool (L) for lasso selection, **Annotate** (D/3) for creating annotations, **Annotate Line** (3/4) for creating a line note, **Annotate Polygon** (4/5) for creating a polygon note, **Annotate Eraser** (5/6) for erasing annotations, and **Links Cut** (6/7) for cutting links.

Note   Once again, the default hotkey for Annotation is **D,** but when you click any annotation tool, its hotkey changes. In this toolbar, the D is replaced by 3. This affects other tools' hotkeys. Be aware of those changes.

Node Editor

The Node Editor is where you edit or create the materials. There are a lot of materials, set by category; it depends on the render engine that you use.

When it comes to the Materials menu under the Input, Texture, Color, Vector, Script, Group, and Layout categories, the three render engines—Eevee, Cycles, and Workbench—have the same list; whereas in the Converter, Output, and Shader categories, there are differences. I won't say much about the Input and Output categories. There are several options, all of which are fairly straightforward.

The small circles that you see beside the nodes are called *sockets*, as shown in Figure 4-14.

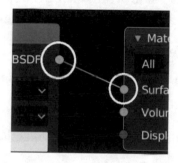

Figure 4-14. *Sockets*

The sockets that are placed on the right side of the nodes are called *output sockets*. The sockets placed on the left side are called the *input sockets*. These sockets are responsible for linking the nodes and transmitting information from one node to another.

Next, I discuss some of the nodes a bit.

Principled BSDF

Principled BSDF combines multiple layers into an easy-to-use node. It is based on the Disney principled model also known as a *PBR shader*. Image textures painted or baked from software like Substance Painter may be likely linked to the corresponding parameters in this shader.

The following are the inputs.

- **Base Color** sets the diffuse/metal surface color.

- **Subsurface** sets the value for mixing the base color and subsurface color.

- **Subsurface Radius** sets the average distance that light scatters below the surface.

- **Subsurface Color** sets the subsurface scattering color.

- **Metallic** sets the Metallic value.

- **Specular** sets the dielectric specular reflection value.

- **Specular tint** sets the value of tints facing the specular reflection using the base color while glancing reflection remains white.

- **Roughness** sets the roughness value.

- **Anisotropic** sets the amount of anisotropy for specular reflection.

- **Anisotropic Rotation** rotates the direction of the anisotropy.

- **Sheen** sets the amount of soft velvet like reflection near edges.

- **Sheen Tint** mixes the white and base color for sheen reflection.

- **Clear Coat** sets extra white specular layer on top of others.

- **Clear Coat Roughness** sets roughness of clearcoat specular.

- **IOR** sets the index of refraction value.

- **Transmission** mixes between fully opaque surface at zero and fully glass like transmission at one.

- **Transmission Roughness** controls roughness used for transmitted light with GGX distribution.

- **Emission** lights emission from the surface.

- **Alpha** controls the transparency of the surface of the surface.

- **Normal** controls the normals of the base layers.

- **Clearcoat Normal** controls the normals of the Clearcoat layer.

- **Tangent** controls the tangent for the Anisotropic layer.

There are also Distribution properties. **GGX is** less physically accurate but faster than multiple-scattering GGX and enables Transmission Roughness input. **Multiple-Scattering GGX** provides energy-conserving results that would otherwise be visible as excessive darkening and takes multiple bounces or scattering events between microfacets into account. **Subsurface Method: Christensen-Burley is** an approximation of physically-based volume scattering; it gives less blurry results than the Cubic and Gaussian functions. **Random Walk** provides the most accurate results for thin and curved objects**.**

Mix Shader

Mix Shader mixes shaders together. Mixing can be used for material layering. Factor input is for nodes that enhance the mixing of shaders, like Layer Weight.

Diffuse BSDF

Diffuse BSDF adds Lambertian or Oren-Nayar diffuse reflection. It has Color input, Roughness input, and Normal input.

Glossy BSDF

Glossy BSDF adds reflections with microfacet distribution; it is mostly used for materials like mirrors and metals.

Emission

Emission adds the Lambertian emission shader. It can be used as a light since it has a luminance effect.

Subsurface Scattering

Subsurface Scattering adds subsurface multiple scattering for materials such as skin, wax, marble, milk, and so forth. Rather than light being reflected off the surface, it penetrates the surface and bounces around internally before being absorbed or leaving the surface at a nearby point.

Image Texture

Image Texture adds an image file as a texture.

Math is part of Converter and performs math operations.

Mapping is part of Vector and transforms an image or procedural textures. You can use this to move, rotate, or scale textures when you connected it to Image Texture.

Texture Coordinate is part of Input and commonly used for the coordinates of textures, typically used as inputs for the vector input for texture nodes.

Mix Node or MixRGB is part of Color and mixes images by working on the individual and corresponding pixels of the two inputs.

Color Ramp is part of Converter and maps values to colors with a gradient.

Fresnel is part of Input and computes how much light is reflected off a layer, and where the rest will be refracted through the layer.

Material Output outputs surface material information to a surface object.

Light Output outputs light information to a light object.

World Output outputs light color information to a scene's world.

Let's now proceed to a sample project. It is best to discuss with examples.

Sample Project

We will not use the Suzanne project this time. You can use a scene that you made, just like the other scenes.

Figure 4-15 shows the scene that I made before I applied any modification to the materials. You'll be able to follow along with any random scene that you create.

Figure 4-15. *Rendered scene in Eevee*

Simple, right? Yes. Let's just do a simple project for this example. All of the examples are rendered in Eevee.

First, I applied a modifier to the Suzanne mesh and sphere but not to the torus, cone, and cylinder. I adjusted their vertices in the mesh pop-up menu settings that **only appear when you add mesh**. So, it's better for you to decide how many vertices that you plan to use beforehand.

Let's start the experiment by adding an image background to your scene. So, you'll use Image Texture.

1. In the Layout workspace, click the plane on the left side.

2. Go to the Material panel in Properties and click New.

3. Go to Subsurface Color and click Image Texture. The settings include a drop-down of the images opened in Blender, a button for creating new image, a button for browsing images on your drive, a drop-down list for setting texture interpolation, a drop-down list for projecting a 2D image on an object with a 3D vector, and a drop-down list for how the image is extrapolated past its original bounds.

4.   Open an image on your drive. Figure 4-16 shows what happens.

Figure 4-16. *Rendered Scene in Eevee after Applying Image Texture in Layout workspace*

No, no, no. That picture is not an editorial mistake. It's really a result of Image Texture for now cause we still not doing one thing to implement this completely, the UV mapping.

UV mapping is a method for translating a 2D image into a 3D object. Well, here's a better explanation: if you want to wrap a present, how do you do it? Our gift wrapper is a plain flat square object. You can think of a gift wrapper as a 2D image. Think of things like a tumbler, plate, cup, and other things around you as 3D objects. When you apply an image texture, you need to wrap it around the 3D object; that's why we have a UV editing workspace. Unfortunately, this subject is not discussed much in this book because it's a bit advanced.

So, now, let's go back to our project. Since you're only going to use Image Texture on the plane, it's easy to wrap it up. Go to the UV Editing workspace, and if you already see your image in the UV editor on the left side of your screen, that's it! But when it comes to very detailed things, this becomes more complicated.

Figure 4-17 shows how to do the UV unwrapping.

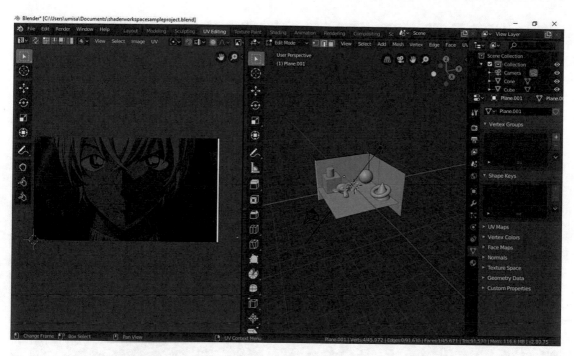

Figure 4-17. *UV uwrapping*

The result is shown in Figure 4-18.

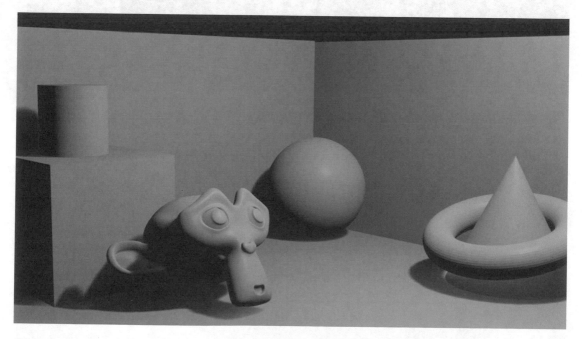

Figure 4-18. *Rendered result with Image Texture and UV Unwrapping*

The image isn't appearing. Why? Well, it's because you didn't adjust the subsurface, which indicates the mixing value between the base color and the subsurface color. Remember that your Image Texture is set to Subsurface Color, and when you look at Figure 4-19, you see in the node editor (in the Shaders workspace) that Image Texture links to the Subsurface color input socket of the Principled BSDF shader. Since your Subsurface value is 0, you're indicating that the color of the base is the top priority, but when you set it to 1, the top priority for the color will be the subsurface color.

Figure 4-19. *Nodes set up in the Shading workspace*

Set the Subsurface to 1, and take a look at Figure 4-20 to see what happened.

Figure 4-20. *Rendered result of the setting Subsurface to 1*

It's already there but wait, the picture is not in the right position. Go back to the UV editor. When you have a texture image, you see white lines around it, which represents the seam or the image placement of the object when 3D is cut to 2D. Select it all and rotate it. Adjust it until you get the result that you want.

Figure 4-21 shows how to do the UV editing.

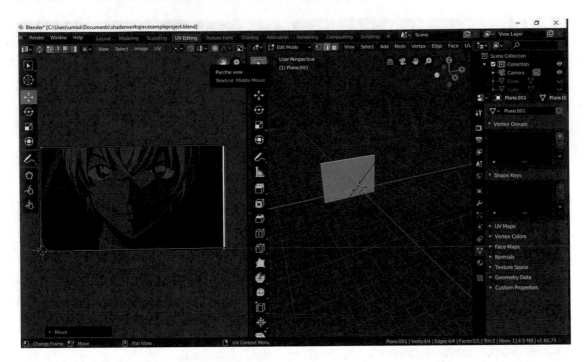

Figure 4-21. *Working with UV editing*

Figure 4-22 shows the new rendered result.

Figure 4-22. *New render result*

Try to add an image texture in the plane on the right side, but instead of using UV editing for positioning the image, use the Mapping node, which is part of the Vector category, and the Texture Coordinate node, which is part of the Input category.

Figure 4-23 shows the node settings for the right plane.

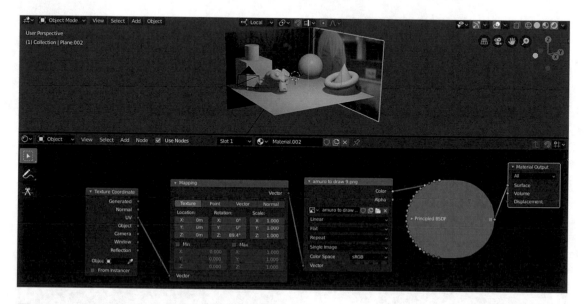

Figure 4-23. *Nodes setting for the right plane*

Choose the texture, which is commonly used when using Mapping for image textures, and set the Z rotation to 89.4 degrees. As you can see in the 3D Viewportat the top, it was already in the desired position. When it was imported, it was in the reversed position. This is like a transformation tool for an image texture. You need to link Mapping to Texture Coordinate's UV output because your basis is the UV of the image texture.

Generated automatically generates texture coordinates from the vertex positions of the mesh without deformation, sticking them to the surface under animation. **Normal** is the normal object space. **Object** is the object as a source for the coordinates. **Camera** positions the coordinates in the camera space. **Window** locates the shading point on the screen. **Reflection** is the direction of the reflection vector as a coordinate.

You might notice that your Principled BSDF shape became oblong. You can see the small triangle in the header of the node. When you click it, it turns the node into an oblong shape. This can be helpful when you want to minimize the space occupied by your node shader.

For the plane in the bottom, delete the Principled BSDF in the node editor and replace it with Emission Shader. You should also add Magic Texture, which adds a psychedelic color texture. I use it to add effects on my materials when I use plain colors.

Set the Emission color to 002990 and its strength to 99.500. Set Magic Texture depth to 5, Scale to 4.800, and Distortion to 0.800. Add two Math nodes and connect them to Scale and Distortion. The following settings are for the Math node you connected in Scale.

- Operation is set to Logarithm.

- Value 1 is set to 0.500.

- Value 2 is set to 0.300.

The settings for the Math node connected in Distortion are as follows.

- Operation is set to Add.

- Value 1 is set to 2.100.

- Value 2 is set to 0.100.

Figure 4-24 shows the node settings for the bottom plane.

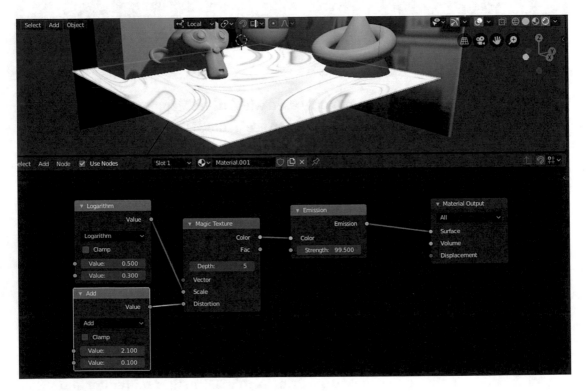

Figure 4-24. *Nodes settings for the bottom plane*

You see the effect of our node setup in the bottom plane. Without Magic Texture and the math node, it was only a plain color. If you remember, you used emission in the Text object in the Suzanne project, and it was plain green. That's only an Emission effect because it is a shader that can be used as a light object. So, unless you connect it with textures and so forth, it will only emit a plain color.

The following is for the Suzanne object.

1. Delete the Principled BSDF and replace it with Diffuse BSDF.

2. Add Glass BSDF and combine the two using the Mix Shader.

3. Add Fresnel node and connect it to Glass BSDF.

4. Set the Diffuse color to E7B354 and Roughness to 0.438.

5. Set the Glass BSDF color to 4907FF, Roughness to 0.508, and Properties to Beckmann.

6. The Fresnel set the IOR to 4.950.

Figure 4-25 shows the Suzanne mesh settings.

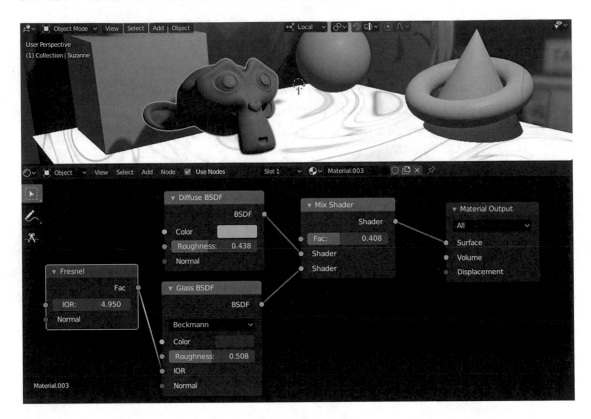

Figure 4-25. *Nodes setting for the Suzanne mesh*

You can use the same nodes settings in the sphere mesh, but in this case, you can group Diffuse BSDF, Mix Shader, and Glass BSDF (see Figure 4-26).

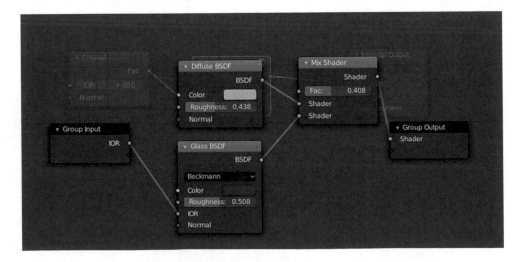

Figure 4-26. *Nodes in groups*

This is the nodes' settings when they are in a group. To go back to the node editor, click the upward arrow in the rightmost side in the Header region of the Shader Editor (see Figure 4-27).

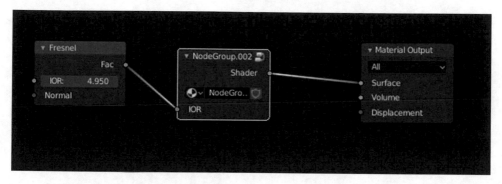

Figure 4-27. *Node setting outside the group*

To ungroup the materials, you need to click the node group. Then go to Node menu ➤ Ungroup or hold Ctrl+Alt+G. To make a group, you need to select the nodes you want to include in the group, then go to Node menu ➤ Make group or press Ctrl+G.

For the cube mesh, use Diffuse BSDF and Glossy BSDF, and add using Add Shader. Connect Color Ramp with Diffuse BSDF and Wave Texture with Glossy BSDF. The following are my settings for this.

- Diffuse color: 0C0FC9 and Diffuse Roughness: 0

- Glossy BSDF color: 00E720, Glossy BSDF Properties: GGX and Glossy BSDF Roughness: 0.500

- ColorRamp Properties: RGB and Linear, ColorRamp Color: FC0500 and 00B3FF, Color Ramp Pos: 1 and Color Ramp Factor: 0.400

- Wave Texture Properties: Bands and Sine, Wave Texture Scale: 7.000, Wave Texture Distortion: 24.700, Wave Texture Detail: 12.300, and Wave Texture Detail Scale: 3.400

Wave Texture adds procedural bands or rings with noise distortion, but personally, I like Magic texture. I use it to add an effect when I think that the shaders are plain.

For the sphere mesh, you can use Diffuse BSDF and Glossy BSDF with Add Shader. I also add MixRGB from the Color category. My settings here are as follows.

- Diffuse BSDF color set to 0C0FC9

- Diffuse BSDF's roughness set to 0.700

- Glossy BSDF color set to 22DAE7

- Glossy BSDF roughness set to 0.492

- Mix Properties set to Multiple

- Mix Factor set to 0.567

- Mix Color1 set to 4567FF

- Mix Color2 set to FF2117

For the cone mesh, you could use the following.

- Diffuse BSDF with a setting of 0018FF for color

- Diffuse BSDF with a setting of E73575 for color

- Diffuse BSDF with a setting of E7E7E7

- Add Shader that connects the last two Diffuse Shaders

- Mix Shader that connects the first Diffuse BSDF to the Add Shader and with a setting of 0.683 in Factor

- Noise Texture that connects to the color of the third Diffuse BSDF and with a setting of 7.500 in Detail and 10.600 for Distortion

- Math node with a setting of Add in properties: 4.500 for the first value and 0.300 for the second

For the cylinder mesh, I suggest the Checker texture. For the torus mesh, the Specular node and Diffuse Shader and mix its value with Mix Shader. Connect the RGB Curves to the Base Color of the Specular Node input and Diffuse BSDF Color input. Also add Gradient texture and connect it to the RGB curves input.

Note Yes, I do love to apply texture nodes to make my shader nodes interesting.

Figure 4-28 shows the node settings for the cube mesh, sphere mesh, and cone mesh.

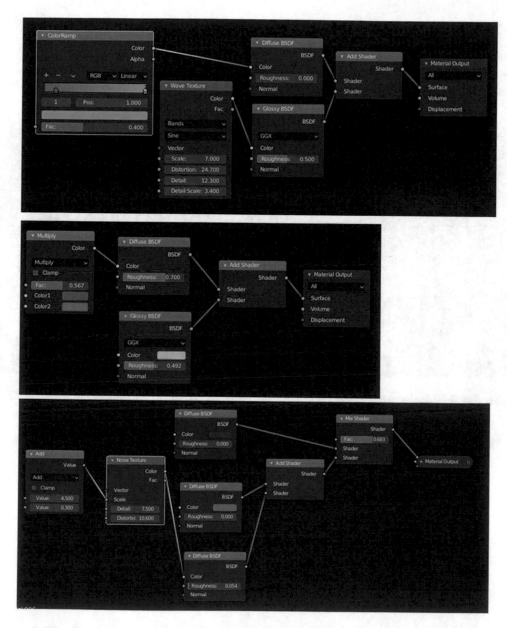

Figure 4-28. *Node settings for cube mesh (upper image), sphere mesh (center image), and cone mesh (bottom image)*

147

Figure 4-29 shows the nodes' settings for cylinder mesh and torus mesh.

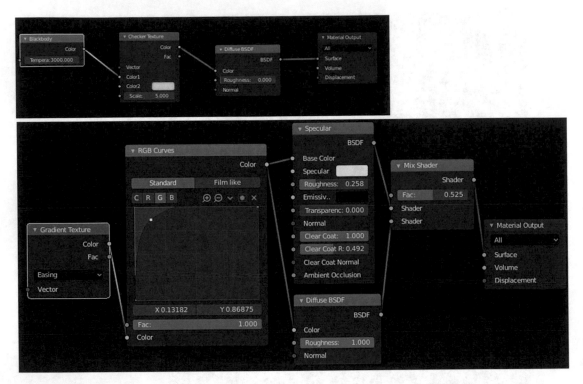

Figure 4-29. *Node setting for cylinder mesh (top) and torus mesh (bottom)*

Figure 4-30 shows the final rendered image.

Figure 4-30. *Rendered Result*

You can adjust the strength of emission to 20 to see more details. I'd like to note, once again, that this is rendered from Eevee.

Other Samples

Before I end this chapter and proceed to the next chapter, where I discuss animation, I'd like you to see some renders by artists on Blenderartist.org (see Figures 4-31 to 4-33).

Figure 4-31. *Church by GBizzle*

Figure 4-32. *Visitors by Victor Duarte*

Figure 4-33.   *Bee by Lucas Falcao*

CHAPTER 5

Let's Animate with Blender

I talked about the Blender user interface in Chapter 1. I talked about the Layout workspace, Modeling workspace, and Shader workspace in Chapters 2, 3, and 4. You even had a sneak peek of the UV editing workspace and many Blender features through sample projects. I also discussed the fundamentals of light and color and the various editors.

The focus of this chapter is the Animation workspace and the Rendering workspace. So, let's start the tour!

Note   As animation is harder to demonstrate on the page, I have not provided sample projects for every topic in this chapter. You'll see plenty of options along the way to allow you to use Blender for your own animations.

Animation Workspace

This workspace is where you can create and edit your animation. This workspace contains 3D Viewport, Outliner, Properties, Dope Sheet, and Timeline.

Figure 5-1 shows this workspace.

© Ezra Thess Mendoza Guevarra 2020
E. T. M. Guevarra, *Modeling and Animation Using Blender*, https://doi.org/10.1007/978-1-4842-5340-3_5

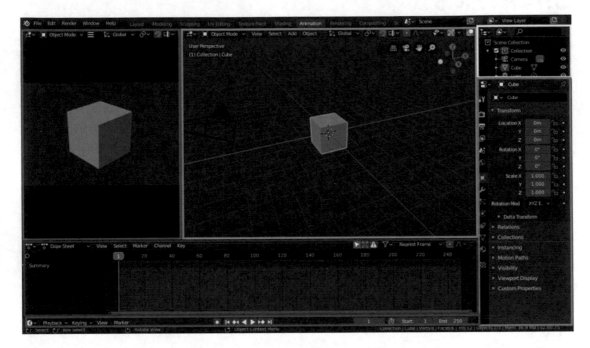

Figure 5-1. *Animation workspace*

Figure 5-1 shows the 3D Viewports. One is in camera perspective, which you can see by pressing 0 in your numpad or by selecting View ➤ Viewpoint ➤ Camera. The other viewport is in its regular settings.

Dope Sheet

Dope Sheets give the animator a bird's-eye view of the keyframes inside the scene. This is inspired by the classical hand-drawn animation process, in which animators use charts, showing exactly when each drawing, sound, and camera move will occur, and for how long. This is also called an *exposure sheet*.

Dope Sheet is divided into three regions: Header region, Channel region, and Main region. It has six modes: Dope Sheet, Action Editor, Shake Key Editor, Grease Pencil, Mask, and Cache File.

Dope Sheet ➤ Dope Sheet Mode

Dope Sheet mode allows you to edit multiple actions at once. By default, this is the mode selected for Dope Sheet. Figure 5-2 shows its settings.

Figure 5-2. *Dope Sheet mode*

The one in inside the blue rectangle, place in the top, is the Header region. The one on the left is the Channel region, and the one on the right is the Main region. It also has a sidebar, but it is hidden by default; you can access it by pressing **N** on your keyboard.

Let's discuss the Header region. On the left is the Select menu for Editor Type. Next to it is the Select menu for Dope Sheet mode. Next are the Header menus, which are View, Select, Marker, Channel, and Key. Then, there are three icons for filtering. **Only Selected** (arrow icon) is for showing/including only the channels related to selected objects and data. **Display Hidden** (small dotted square) is for showing/including the channels from objects or bones that are not visible **Show Errors** (exclamation point inside a triangle) is for showing/including F-curves and drivers that are disabled or have errors.

Figure 5-3 shows a simple F-curves demonstration.

Figure 5-3. *Simple demonstration*

For example, you wanted to animate those three arrows. To animate, elements called **Keyframes** allow you to tell the software, "This is how big the arrow is. This is where the arrow is at this moment." But there is a problem. If I want to make a too big arrow to medium arrow, then too small arrow, will I repeatedly assign keyframes? I use keyframes to indicate the movement of my animation. This is where the **F-curves** come in. When you create set a keyframe from one end to another to create an animation, it creates an **F-curves** or a line that you can move for an effect for your animation. This helps you lessen your efforts with repeatedly creating keyframes and from preventing multiple keyframes. Let's go back to the Header region.

Frame defines increments on the Timeline/Dope Sheet/Graph Editor. The number, seconds, and so forth. The part of the timeline where your animation runs is the frame. Think of it as a time frame. That is the time frame that you allotted your animation. Remember, we can assign or set where the frame will start and end through the playback pop-over menu.

Keyframe is a frame where a change occurs in the Timeline/Dope Sheet/Graph Editor. It's an indication that changes happen in this part of frame. F-curves lessen the usage of keyframes.

Let's go back to the traditional animation. The animation where animators use paper and they flip it to perform an action for you to easily imagine this part. If you have the whole pad of paper, think of it as the frame. Since it is traditional, paper and pencil are used, think of the paper as the keyframes. Imagine how many times you need to move, re-create you object, move a small detail to have a single object animate. It cost you a lot when doing it. That's why when animation are digitized, in 2D animation they create this so called Motion Tween that links two key frame that is apart. You need to create a big circle and insert a keyframe then leave frames apart insert another keyframe where you draw a small circle and you will see when you play it, it automatically animate the big circle turning to small circle. Magic? Well, the magic of math and technology. This Motion Tween is the same as F-Curves.

Let's go back to the Dope Sheet Header region.

Next to the three icons is the Filtering pop-up menu. Figure 5-4 shows what's in it.

Figure 5-4. *Filters*

From the top, there is **Summary**, which is enabled by default. This is the summary in the Channel region. **Only Selected** is enabled by default. Next are **Display Hidden** and **Show Errors**. As you can see, these settings are for enabling/disabling or showing/hiding element. In Show Errors is a search box called Name Filters. This name filters can be seen also in Channel region. In these settings are the Filter Types. This filter types help you choose what to include in visualization related to animation data.

Next is the Select menu for the snapping tool. There are six options. **No Auto Snap** means no snapping at all. **Frame Step** means snap to 1.0 frame intervals. **Second Step** means snap to 1.0 second intervals. **Nearest Frame** means snap to actual frames. **Nearest Second** means snap to actual seconds. **Nearest Marker** means snap to nearest marker. By default, it is set to Nearest Frame.

Last is the Proportional Editing Falloff. There are eight options: Random, Constant, Linear, Sharp, Inverse Square, Root, Sphere, and Smooth.

Dope Sheet Mode Header Menus

There is View, Select, Marker, Channel, and Key.

Figure 5-5 shows the command in these Header menus.

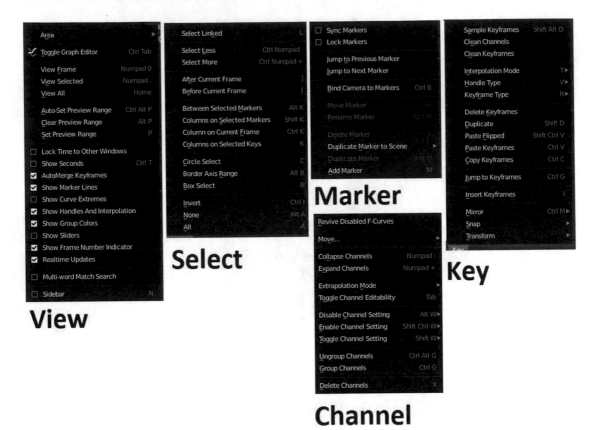

Figure 5-5. Dope Sheet mode Header menus

Figure 5-5 is taken when I still don't have anything in the Dope Sheet. In the Marker menu, some commands are disabled. It's because there are no markers in the Dope Sheet. Most Marker commands only work when your cursor is in the marker itself or when you hover your cursor to the marker, even when using shortcut keys.

The View and Select menus are very straightforward, so you can refer to Figure 5-5 for the hotkeys.

Markers Menu

What are Markers? What exactly its purpose? Markers denote frames with key points or significant events within an animation. Example, it could be that a character animation starts, the camera changes position, lighting on change it color or a cube moves it position. Markers can be given names to make them more meaningful at a quick glance. Unlike keyframes, markers are always placed at a whole framed number. You cannot set a marker at frame 2.5.

Let's discuss what's in the Markers menu. **Sync Markers** syncs markers with keyframe edits. **Lock Markers** prevents marker editing. **Jump To Previous Markers** jumps to previous marker from the current marker selected. **Jump to Next Markers** jumps to next marker from the current marker selected. **Bind Camera to Markers** (Ctrl+B) binds the selected camera to a marker on a current frame, and in this way, the operator allows markers to set the active object as the active camera. **Move Markers** (G) moves selected time marker. **Rename Markers** (Ctrl+M) renames first selected marker. **Delete Markers** (X) deletes selected time marker. **Duplicate Marker to Scene** copies selected marker to another scene. **Duplicate Marker** (Shift+D) duplicates selected marker and **Add Marker** (M) adds a new time marker.

Channel Menu

Let's discuss the Channel menu. **Revive Disabled F-Curves** clears the disabled tag from all F-curves to get broken F-curves working again. **Move** rearranges selected animation channels. There are four options: To Top (Shift+Page Up), Up (Page Up), Down (Page Down), and To Bottom (Shift Page Down). **Collapse Channel** (Numpad-) collapses all selected expandable animation channels. **Expand Channel** (Numpad+) expands all selected expandable animation channels. **Extrapolation mode** sets extrapolation mode for selected F-curves. There are four options: Constant Extrapolation, Linear Extrapolation, Make Cyclic (F-Modifier), and Clear Cyclic (F-Modifier).

Let's discuss Extrapolation mode. Extrapolation defines the behavior of a curve before the first and after the last keyframes. **Constant Extrapolation** is the default one. It curves before the first keyframe and the last one has a constant value. **Linear Extrapolation** has curved ends that are straight lines as defined by their first two keyframes (respectively, their last two keyframes). Make Cyclic and Clear Cyclic are for **F-modifiers**, which are similar to object modifiers, in that they add non-destructive effects, that can be adjusted at any time, and layered to create complex effects. This can be found when you are using Graph Editor.

In the Channel menu, we also have **Toggle Channel Editability** (Tab) toggles editability of selected channels. **Disable Channel Setting** (Alt+W) disables specified setting on all selected animation channels. There are two options: Protect and Mute. **Enable Channel Setting** (Shift+Ctrl+W) enables a specified setting on all selected animation channels. There are two options: Protect and Mute. **Toggle Channel Setting** (Shift+W) toggles specified setting on all selected animation channels. There are two options: Protect and Mute. **Ungroup Channel** (Ctrl+Alt+G) removes selected F-curves from their current groups. **Group Channels** (Ctrl+G) adds selected F-curves to a new group. **Delete Channels** (X) deletes all selection animation channels.

Key Menu

Let's discuss the Key menu. **Sample Keyframes** (Shift+Alt+O) adds keyframes on every frame between the selected keyframes. **Clean Channels/Clean Keyframes** simplifies F-curves by removing closely spaced keyframes. **Interpolation mode** (T) sets the interpolation mode for the F-curve segments starting from the selected keyframes. There are 13 options divided into three categories. In Interpolation, there is Constant, Linear, and Bezier. In Easing, there is Sinusoidal, Quadratic, Cubic, Quartic, Quintic, Exponential, and Circular. In Dynamic Effects, there is Back, Bounce, and Elastic. Let's discuss this a bit.

Interpolation mode is a mode for interpolation, or process calculating new data between points known as value, between the current and next playframe. There are 13 options available.

- **Constant** means there is no interpolation at all. The curve holds the value of its last keyframe, giving a discrete curve. Usually only used during the initial blocking stage in pose-by-pose animation.

- **Linear** is a simple interpolation creates a straight segment, giving a non-continuous line. It can be useful when using only two keyframes.

- **Bezier** is the more powerful and useful interpolation, and the default one. It gives nicely smoothed curves.

- **Back** is cubic easing with overshoot and settle. Use this one when you want a bit of an overshoot coming into the next keyframe, or perhaps for some wind-up anticipation.

- **Bounce** is exponentially decaying parabolic bounce like when objects collide.

- **Elastic** is exponentially decaying sine wave like an elastic band. This is like bending a stiff pole stuck to some surface, and watching it rebound and settle back to its original state.

The options under Easing are different methods for easing interpolations for F-curve segments. The Robert Penner Easing Equations are equations that define preset ways that one keyframe transitions to another, which reduce the amount of manual work, the inserting and tweaking keyframes, to achieve certain common effects.

The Easing is the transition from one key frame to the next. When you are in the Graph Editor and you added a keyframes, and changed the Easing options, the curves of the Graph Editor change pretty dramatically.

Again, you can switch to Graph Editor by going to View ➤ Toggle Graph Editor or hold Ctrl+Tab. Figure 5-6 shows the Graph Editor after toggling from Dope Sheet.

Figure 5-6. *Graph Editor*

Each of the Easing mode plays with the curve of a keyframe. Before the key, we called it Easing in, and after the key, we called it Easing Out.

Let's talk a bit about the Easing (by Strength) options.

The term **Sinusoidal** refers to the Sinusoid, which is a mathematical curve. This Easing mode creates a curve that eases in sharply and gradually eases out. It gives each keyframe a look of impact. It starts quickly and ends abruptly. After you select **Quadratic**, it looks like Sinusoidal. Besides its name in the options, there are numbers in it, as you can see in Figure 5-7. These options with the numbered icon are going to increase the effect mentioned in Sinusoidal. They ease in and ease out gradually, which has an increasing sense of build that is very useful in some actions. **Cubic Quartic and Quintic** becomes progressively punchier until you get to Quintic and have a hit that seems to fly out of nowhere, but is on the edge of being unrealistic.

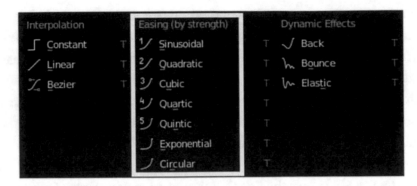

Figure 5-7. *Intepolation mode Options*

If you want to create reactive animations (like a fight scene), you can use these five modes.

Exponential moves into the realm of unrealistic acceleration. If you wanted to do a slow motion effect that gradually moves closer to some keyed action and they hits suddenly and all at once while **Circular** basically abandons easing in and teleports before easing out again. This is well beyond unrealistic. This is well beyond unrealistic, and so it can be used in all manner or cartoonish styles to make some incredibly quick movements. Just be mindful about this mode's impact looking fake or weightless.

These modes affect the animation quite differently if your easing type is set to Ease Out or Ease In and Out. You can right-click in the Graph Editor or press Ctrl+E to change the Easing type.

I provide a site where you can found a live demo and link to an ebook that explains more about the options for Easing for you to learn more: `http://robertpenner.com/easing/`.

Next, let's consider **Handle Type** (V), which sets type of handle for selected keyframe. There are five options: Free, Aligned, Vector, Automatic, and Auto Clamped. **Free** breaks handle tangents. **Aligned** handle maintain rotation when moved and curved tangent is maintained. **Vector** creates linear interpolation between keyframes. The linear segments remain if keyframe centers are moved. If handles are moved the handle becomes Free. **Automatic** keyframes are automatically interpolated. **Auto Clamped** auto handles clamped to not overshoot.

Using **Keyframe Type** (R) sets type of keyframe for the selected keyframe. There are five options: Keyframe, Breakdown, Moving, Hold Extreme, and Jitter. **Keyframe** (white/yellow diamond) is a normal keyframe. **Breakdown** (small cyan diamond) is the breakdown state; for example, transition between key poses. **Moving Hold** (dark gray/orange diamond) is a keyframe that adds a small amount of motion around a holding pose and in Dope Sheet, it also displays a bar between them. **Extreme** (big pink diamond) an extreme state or some other purpose as needed. **Jitter** (tiny green diamond) a filler or baked keyframe for keying on ones or some other purpose as needed.

The **Delete Keyframes Duplicate** (Shift+D), **Paste Flipped** (Shift+Ctrl+V), **Paste Keyframes** (Ctrl+V), **Copy Keyframes** (Ctrl+C), **Jump to Keyframes** (Ctrl+G), and **Insert Keyframes** (I) are straightforward. More interesting is **Mirror (Ctrl+M)** flips selected keyframes over the selected mirror line. There are three options.

- **By Times Over Current Frame** flips times of selected keyframes using the current frame as the mirror line.

- **By Values over Value** flips values of selected keyframes; for example, negative values becomes positive or vice versa.

- **By Times over First Selected Marker** flips times of selected keyframes using the first selected marker as the reference point.

Snap is also quite useful; it snaps selected keyframes to the times specified. There are four options.

- **Current frame** snaps selected keyframes to the current frame.

- **Nearest Frame** snaps selected keyframes to the nearest frame.

- **Nearest Second** snaps selected keyframes to the nearest second.

- **Nearest Marker** snaps selected keyframes to the nearest marker.

Finally, **Transform** transforms selected items by mode type. There are four options. **Move** (G) moves a single keyframe. **Extend** (E) extends the time between two keys. **Slide** (Shift+T) slides selected keyframes. **Scale** (S) scales selected keyframes.

You will learn more about this through sample projects.

Dope Sheet ➤ Action Editor Mode

Action Editor is where you can define and control actions. It enables you to view and edit the f-Curve data-blocks you defined as Actions in the F-Curve Editor.

It gives you a slightly simplified view of the F-Curve data-blocks. The editor can list all Action data-blocks of an object at once.

Each Action data-block forms a top-level channel. Note that an object can have several constraints (one per animated constraint) and pose (for armatures, one per animated bone) F-curve data-blocks, and hence an action can have several of these channels.

Figure 5-8 shows the default setup of this mode.

Figure 5-8. *Dope Editor ➤ Action Editor mode*

The Channel region has few a differences in the Dope Sheet. The **Summary** isn't shown in the Channel region here but the **Name Filter** is.

In the Header region, the Channel menu isn't seen but the View, Select, Marker, and Key header menus are. The commands inside these header menus are the same. What you can see in **Filters** also differs. Figure 5-9 shows what's available in the Filters of this mode.

Figure 5-9. *Action Editor mode ➤ Filters*

Wait a minute. Summary is enabled. How come that it isn't shown in the Channel region? It's because it only shows when you already have animation or actions to edit.

Figure 5-10 shows a summary in Action Editor mode.

Figure 5-10. *Action Editor mode ➤ Summary*

See that after I add keyframes or simple animation, Summary appeared in the Channel region. The Header region has an up/down arrow. This is for switching to editing action in animation layer below or above the current action in the NLA stack. Next to it are the Push Down button and Stash button. **Push down** is to push action down on the NLA stack as a new strip while the **Stash** stores the selected action in the NLA stack as a non-contributing strip for later use. The up/down arrows, Push down, and Stash button are disabled since we're not using the NLA or Non-Linear Animation Editor.

What is NLA? Non-Linear Animation (NLA) is an animation technique that allows the animator to edit motions as a whole, not as the individual keys. Non-Linear animations allow you to combine, mix, and blend different motions to create entirely new animations.

I'd like to note also that once you push down or stash, you can't select either action since it's been sent to the NLA. A stashed action can be edited but you cannot add keyframes anymore.

So, let's go back to the header region. You can also see that in the Header region, there is something called CubeAction. CubeAction is the name of the F-curves for the animation that you made. The rectangle represents the list of actions created for the objects. You can also view it by clicking the icon beside the rectangle. The Proportional Editing Falloff list is the same and so is the snapping.

Dope Sheet ➤ Shape Key Editor Mask and Cache File Mode

Shape Key Editor adjusts the animation timing of shape keys. These are stored inside an Action data-block. It lets you edit the value of relative shape keys.

Shape Keys animate deform objects into new shapes. They can be applied on objects with vertices like Mesh, Curves, Surfaces, and Lattice. There are two types of Shape Keys: Relative, which is relative to the basis or selected shape key, and Absolute, which is relative to the previous and next shape key.

Figure 5-11 shows this mode.

Figure 5-11. *Dope Sheet ➤ Shape Key Editor*

Yeah. It has the same setup as the Action Editor with a different purpose because it is specifically for editing shape keys.

Mask mode is where you can edit and select the mask shape key frames. All mask data-blocks in blend file are shown. Figure 5-12 shows its setup.

Figure 5-12. *Dope Sheet ➤ Mask mode*

As you can see, there is nothing much here aside from the Summary and Name filter in the Channel region, the View menu, Select menu, Marker menu, Key menu, Filters, Snapping and Proportional Editing Falloff for the Header region because it is specifically for editing mask data-blocks. **Mask** is a grayscale image that included or excluded parts of an image. A matte is applied as an alpha channel or it is used as a mix factor when applying color blend modes.

Masks can be created in the UV/Image and Movie Clip Editors, by changing the mode to Mask in the header. Masks have many purposes. They can be used in a motion tracking workflow to mask out, or influence a particular object in the footage. They can be used for manual rotoscoping to pull a particular object out of the footage, or as a rough matte for green-screen keying. Masks are independent from a particular image of movie clip, and so they can just as well be used for creating motion graphics or other effects in the compositor. Mask data-blocks contain multiple mask layers and splines. They are the most high-level entities used for masking purposes. Masks can be reused in different places, and hold global parameters for all entities they consist of.

Let's proceed to the **Cache File mode**. This mode edits timings for Cache File data-blocks.

Figure 5-13 shows this mode.

Figure 5-13. *Dope Sheet ➤ Cache File mode*

Cache File mode looks like the Dope Sheet mode. It only differs on its use. This is a new mode developed by the team. This Cache File mode is for working with Alembic files.

What is Alembic? Alembic is an open computer graphics interchange framework. Alembic distills complex, animated scenes into a non-procedural, application-independent set of baked geometric results. This distillation of scenes into baked geometry is exactly analogous to the distillation of lighting and rendering scenes into rendered image data.

Alembic is focused on efficiently storing the computed results of complex procedural geometric constructions. It is very specifically not concerned with storing the complex dependency graph procedural tools to create the computed results.

To simplify it, Cache File mode edits the Blender cache file. It is quite technical. The simplest way I can tell about this is it is a temporary file stored in your computer for your file as a backup.

Dope Sheet ➤ Grease Pencil Mode

Grease Pencil allows you to adjust the timing of the grease pencil tool's animated sketches. It is especially useful for animators blocking out shots, where the ability to re-time blocking is one of the main purpose of the whole exercise.

Figure 5-14 shows this mode.

Figure 5-14. *Dope Editor ➤ Grease Pencil mode*

The Channel region of this mode has Summary and the Name filter. The Header region has the View menu, Select menu, Marker menu, Channel menu, and Frame menu.

The **Active Only** button only shows Grease Pencil data-blocks used as part of the active scene.

The Channel region of the Grease Pencil shows the data-blocks containing the layers. Multiple blocks are used for each area. This channel contains the keyframes to which the layer binds.

It is also possible to copy sketches from a layer to other layers using the Copy and Paste buttons. This works in a similar way as copy/paste tools for keyframes in the Action Editor.

Sketches can also be copied from data-block to another using these tools. It is important to keep in mind that keyframes will only be pasted into selected layers, so layers need to be created for the destination areas too.

Insert Keyframe can be used for creating blank Grease Pencil frames at a particular frame. It will create blank frames if Additive Drawing is disabled; otherwise, it makes a copy of the active frame on that layer, and use that.

Grease Pencil Mode Header Menus

Figure 5-15 shows the commands under the Grease Pencil mode's Header menus.

Figure 5-15. Grease Pencil mode's Header menus

In Figure 5-15, only View and Marker menu remains the same. There are changes in Select menu, Channel menu and Frame menu.

Let's discuss the three channels, starting with the Select menu.

After Current Frame (]) selects the keyframe after the current frame. **Before Current Frame** ([) selects the keyframe before the current frame. **Between Selected Markers** (Alt+K) selects all keyframes between selected markers. **Columns on Selected Markers** (Shift+K) selects all keyframes on selected markers. **Column on Current Frame** (Ctrl+K) selects all keyframes on current frame. **Columns on Selected Keys** (K) selects all keyframes on selected keys. **Circle Select** (C) selects keyframes using circle select. **Border Axis Range** (Alt+B) selects all keyframes within the specific region. **Box Select** (B) selects keyframes using box select. **Invert** (Ctrl+I) selects keyframes using inverse selection. **None** (Alt+A) deselects all currently selected keyframes. **All** (A) selects all keyframes.

What differs with this Select menu is that it doesn't have Select Linked, Select Less, and Select More.

CHAPTER 5   LET'S ANIMATE WITH BLENDER

Let's proceed to the Channel menu. **Delete Channels** (X) deletes all selection animation channels. **Toggle Channel Setting** (Shift+W) toggles specified setting on all selected animation channels. There are two options that appear after you click the command: Protect and Mute. **Enable Channel Setting** (Shift+Ctrl+W) enables specified setting on all selected animation channels. There are two options that appear after you click the command: Protect and Mute. **Disable Channel Setting** (Alt+W) disables specified setting on all selected animation channels. There are two options that appear after you click the command: Protect and Mute. **Toggle Channel Editability** (Tab) toggles editability of selected channels.

What differs between this channel menu to the previous ones are this doesn't have Revive Disabled F-Curve, Move, Collapse Channels, Expand Channels, Extrapolation mode, Ungroup Channel, and Group Channel.

Let's discuss the Frame menu.

- **Transform** transforms selected items. There are four options: Move (G), Extend (E), Slide (Shift+T), and Scale (S). **Move** moves selected items. **Extend** extends selected items. **Slide** slides selected items. **Scale** scales or resize selected items.

- **Snap** snaps selected keyframes to the times specified. There are four options. **Current Frame** snaps selected keyframes to the current frame. **Nearest Frame** snaps selected keyframes to the nearest frame. **Nearest Second** snaps selected keyframes to the nearest second. **Nearest Marker** snaps selected keyframes to the nearest marker.

- **Mirror** (Ctrl+M) flips selected keyframes over the selected mirror line. There are three options. **By Times over Current Frame** flips times of selected keyframes using the current frame as the mirror line. **By Values over Value = 0** flips the values of selected keyframes example negative turn to positive or vice versa. **By Times over First Selected Marker** flips the time of selected keyframes using the first selected marker as the reference point.

- **Duplicate Keyframes** makes a copy of all selected keyframes. **Delete Keyframes** remove all selected keyframes. **Set Keyframe Type** (R) sets type of keyframes for the selected keyframes by clicking the command and the option will pop up.

Timeline

Timeline is located at the bottom of the Animation workspace. Timeline gives the user a broad overview of a scene's animation, by showing the current frame, the keyframes of the active object, the start and end frames of your animation sequence, as well as markers set by the user.

Figure 5-16 shows the timeline in the Animation workspace.

Figure 5-16. *The look of Timeline in Animation workspace*

Is that only the timeline? Well, by default, that is only what is shown in the Animation workspace, but you can see its entire setup by hovering your mouse cursor in the top part of your timeline. When you see the double-sided arrow, drag it up. You will see a setting similar to Figure 5-17.

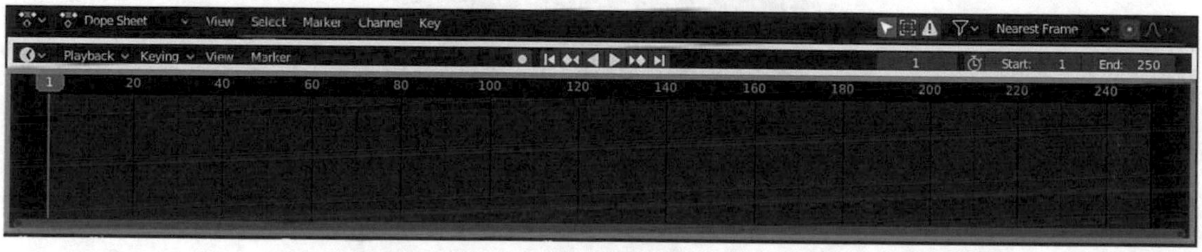

Figure 5-17. *Timeline Editor at its full setup*

You can only see the Dope Sheet Header region because the Timeline occupies the space of the Channel region and Main region of the Dope Sheet as we resize it. This is not specific for timeline. This is applied to all editors when you drag or resize an editor and extend it to the side of the other editor.

So let's go back to the timeline. Figure 5-17 shows the default Timeline setup. By default, the Channel region is hidden, but you can make it appear by placing you mouse cursor on the small arrow next to the timeline; when your cursor turns to a double-sided arrow, drag it to the right.

Below the Header region is the Timeline region, where you see the animation flow. In the Header region, there are Playback, Keying, View, and Marker menus and Transport controls.

Figure 5-18 shows the Playback pop-up menu.

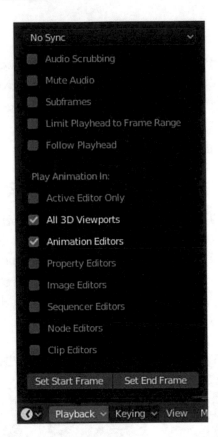

Figure 5-18. *Playback pop-over menu*

The Playback pop-over menu contains options for controlling animation playback. **Sync mode** synchronizes the playback if the scene is detailed and playback is slower than the set frame rate. This is shown in the 3D Viewport when you play the animation. There are three options. **No Sync** means no synchronization happens. **Frame Dropping** means drops frames when the playback is too slow. **AV-Sync or Audio/Video Synchronization** means to sync audio clock and drops frames when playback is slow.

Audio Scrubbing plays bits of the sound wave while you move the playhead with the left mouse button or keyboard arrow keys if your animation has sound. **Mute Audio** mutes sound from any audio source. **Subframes** displays and allows changing the current scene sub-frame. **Limit Playhead to Frame Range** doesn't allow selecting frames outside of the playback range using the mouse. **Follow Playhead** follows current frame in the editors. **Active Editor Only** updates the Timeline while playing if the *Animation Editors* and *All 3D* Viewports are disabled. **All 3D Viewports** updates the 3D Viewport and the timeline while playing. **Animation Editors** updates the Timeline,

Dope Sheet, Graph Editor, and Video Sequencer. **Property Editors** updates the property values in the UI while the animation is playing. **Image Editors** is the Image Editor in Mask mode. **Sequencer Editors** updates the Video sequencer while the animation is playing. **Node Editors** updates the Node Properties while the animation is playing. **Clip Editors** updates the Movie Clip Editor. **Set Start Frame** a button where you can use to choose where part of the timeline region you want to set your Start Frame. **Set End Frame** button allows you to choose where in the timeline region you want to set your end frame.

Now, let's proceed to the Keying pop-over menu. Figure 5-19 shows this pop-over menu.

Figure 5-19. *Keying Pop-over menu*

The Keying pop-over menu contains options that affect keyframe insertion. With **Active Keying Set,** the keying sets are a set of keyframe channels in one. They are made so the user can record multiple properties at the same time. With a keying set selected, when you insert a keyframe, Blender will add keyframes for the properties in the active Keying Set. There are two small buttons with keys in its icons. **Insert Keyframes** inserts keyframes on the current frame for the properties in the active set. **Delete Keyframes** deletes keyframes on the current frame for the properties in the active set.

New Keyframe Type inserts keyframe types. There are five options. **Keyframe** is a normal keyframe. **Breakdown** is the breakdown state that mostly for transitions between key poses. **Moving Hold** is a keyframe that adds a small amount of motion around a holding pose. **Extreme** is an extreme state. Jitter is a filler and baked keyframe for keying on ones. **Auto-Keyframing mode** controls how the auto keyframe mode works.

There are two options. **Add & Replace** adds or replaces existing keyframes. **Replace** replaces existing keyframes. **Auto Keying Set** the one with two keys icon. **Auto Keyframe** inserts new keyframes for the properties in the active Keying Set. **Layered Recording** adds a new NLA Track and strip for every loop/pass made over the animation to allow non-destructive tweaking. **Cycle-Aware Keying applies** special handling to preserve the cycle integrity when inserting keyframes into trivially cyclic curves.

Figure 5-20 shows what's in the View menu of the Timeline.

Figure 5-20. *Timeline ➤ View menu*

Let's discuss the View menu. **Area** allows you to choose how the editor is displayed. There are five options: Horizontal Split, Vertical Split, Duplicate Area into New Window, Toggle Maximize Area (Ctrl+spacebar), and Toggle Fullscreen Area (Ctrl+Alt+spacebar). **View Frame** (Numpad 0) resets viewable area to show range around current frame. **View All** (Home) resets viewable area to show full keyframe range. **Cache** gives you an option to show caches. There are seven options: Show Cache, Softbody, Particles, Cloth, Smoke, Dynamic Paint, and Rigid Body.

What is a cache? It is a block of memory for temporary storage of data likely to be used again. It is made up of a pool of entries. Each entry has associated data, which is a copy of the same data in some backing store. To put it simply, it is data that is saved to be used again. This is how Cache works; it makes your usual tasks easy.

OK, let's go back to the View menu. **Only Keyframes from Selected Channels** considers keyframes for active Object and/or its selected bones only. **Show Frame Number Indicator** shows the frame number beside the current frame indicate line. **Show Marker Lines** shows a vertical line for every marker. **Lock Time to Other Windows** synchronizes the horizontal panning and scale of the current editor with the other editors and this way you always have these editors (Graph Editor, Dope Sheet, NLA) showing an identical part of time you work on. **Show Seconds** (Ctrl+T) shows the time in the x axis and the playhead as frames or as seconds.

Let's discuss the Marker menu in the timeline. Figure 5-21 shows what's inside this menu.

Figure 5-21. *Timeline ➤ Marker menu*

As you can see in the Marker menu, there are commands that are disabled. It's because there are no markers in the Timeline. Most of the Marker's command will only work when your cursor are in the marker itself or when you hover your cursor to the marker, even when using shortcut keys.

Lock Markers prevents marker editing. **Jump to Previous Marker** jumps to previous marker from the current marker selected. **Jump to Next Marker** jumps to next marker from the current marker selected. **Bind Camera to Markers** (Ctrl+B) binds the selected camera to a marker on a current frame; and in this way, the operator allows markers to set the active object as the active camera. **Move Marker** (G) moves selected time marker. **Rename Marker** (Ctrl+M) renames first selected marker. **Delete Marker** (X) deletes selected time marker. **Duplicate Marker to Scene** copies selected marker to another scene. **Duplicate Marker** (Shift+D) duplicates selected marker. **Add Marker** adds a new time marker.

Let's talk about the Transport controls. Figure 5-22 shows this control closely.

Figure 5-22. *Transport Control and Playhead*

These buttons and transport controls set, play, and rewind the playhead. The playhead is the blue vertical line (see Figure 5-22); the current frame number is at the top.

Let's discuss the Transport controls. **Auto Keyframe** adds and/or replaces existing keyframes for the active object when you transform it in the 3D Viewport. **Jump to start** sets the cursor to the start of frame range. **Jump to Previous Keyframe** sets the cursor to the previous keyframe. **Rewind** plays the animation sequence in reverse. When playing the play buttons switch to a pause button. **Play** plays the animation sequence. Again when playing the play buttons switch to a pause button. **Jump to Next Keyframe** sets the cursor to the next keyframe. **Jump to End** sets the cursor to the end of frame range. **Pause** stops the animation.

Figure 5-23 shows the Frame controls.

Figure 5-23. *Frame Controls*

Current Frame is the first rectangle; it shows the current frame and the position of the playhead. **Preview Range is** the clock icon; it is a temporary frame range used for previewing a smaller part of the full range. The preview range only affects the viewport not the rendered output. **Start Frame** shows the starts frame of the animation or playback range. **End Frame** shows the end frame of the animation or playback range.

Graph Editor

The Graph Editor allows users to adjust animation curves over time for any animatable property. It also has three main parts: Main region, Header and Sidebar region, like Dope Sheet Editor and Timeline. Let's discuss its basic settings or common settings.

Figure 5-24 shows the default setup of this editor.

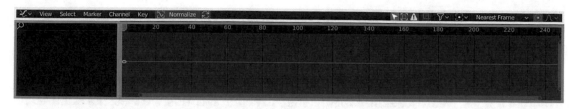

Figure 5-24. *Graph Editor (Header region , yellow; Channel region, green; Main region, light blue)*

In Figure 5-24, the sidebar is hidden by default. You can bring it up by pressing N in your keyboard.

The following are in the Header region of the View menu, Select menu, Marker menu, Channel menu, and Key menu.

- **The Normalize button** normalizes curves so the maximum or minimum point equals 1.0 or –1.0.

- **Only Selected** (the arrow icon) only includes curves related to the selected objects and data.

- **Display Hidden** (the dashed small box icon) includes curves from bones/objects that aren't visible.

- **Show Errors** (the warning triangle icon) only includes curves and drivers that are disabled or have errors. You can select the three at once.

- **Create Ghost Curves** creates snapshot of selected F-curves as background aid for active Graph Editor.

- **Filters** (the funnel icon) a pop-over menu where you can set what data-block to show in the Graph Editor. The Filters are the same as Dope Sheet mode.

- **Pivot Point** where you set the pivot point for the rotation. There are three options: Bounding Box Center, 2D cursor, and Individual Center.

- **Bounding Box Center** is the center of the selected keyframes.

- **2D cursor** is the center of the 2D cursor. It is Playhead+the cursor.

- **Individual Centers** rotates the selected keyframe Bezier handles.

In the Graph Editor, there is a **Snapping** tool. There are six options: No Auto snap, Frame Step, Second Step, Nearest Frame, Nearest Second, and Nearest Marker.

No Auto Snap means no snapping at all. **Frame Step** means snap to 1.0 frame intervals. **Second Step** means snap to one-second intervals. **Nearest Frame** means snap to actual frames. **Nearest Second** means snap to actual seconds. **Nearest Marker** means snap to nearest marker. By default, it is set to Nearest Frame.

Proportional Editing Falloff has eight options: Random, Constant, Linear, Sharp, Inverse Square, Root, Sphere, and Smooth.

Let's discuss the Header menus for the Graph Editor. Figure 5-25 shows what's inside the Header menus.

Figure 5-25. *Header menus for Graph Editor*

View Menu

The View menu of the Graph Editor have that the View menu of Dope Sheet doesn't have. **Only Selected Keyframes Handles** only shows and edit handles of selected keyframes. **Only Selected Curve Keyframes** only keyframes of selected F-curves are visible and editable. **Show Handles** (Ctrl+H) shows the handles of Bezier control points. **Use High Quality Display** displays F-curve using anti-aliasing and other fancy effects. Shows **2D cursor** command shows a 2d cursor. When you used it, you will notice a change in the line of the Graph Editor.

Dope Sheet has Show Curve Extreme, Show Handles, and Interpolation and Multi-word Match Search that the Graph Editor's View menu doesn't have.

In Figure 5-25, most of the commands, especially in Select menu, are disabled. This is because there is nothing in the Graph Editor to work on.

Select Menu

The only difference between the Graph Editor's and Dope Sheet's Select menu is **Border Include Handles**. It selects all keyframes within the specified region.

Marker Menu

For Marker menu, the only difference between Graph Editor and Dope Sheet is that the Sync Marker isn't available in Graph Editor Marker menu. I'd like to note again that Markers denote frames with key points or significant events within an animation.

Channel Menu

We can see that the Graph Editor's Channel menu have Collapse Channel, Expand Channel, Reveal Curves, Hide Unselected Curves, Hide Selected Curves. Dope Sheet's Channel menu doesn't have them, but all of what you can see in its menu is carried.

I'd like to remind you that Extrapolation defines the behavior of a curve before the first and after the last keyframes while Interpolation mode is a mode for interpolation, or process calculating new data between points known as value, between the current and next playframe.

Key Menu

The difference between the Key menu of Graph Editor and the Dope Sheet are the Discontinuity Euler Filter, Bake Curve, Smooth Keys, Easing Type, Bake Sound to F-curves and Add F-curves Modifiers of Graph Editor and Key Frame type of the Dope Sheet.

Sample Project

As usual, this is a step-by-step procedure. Let's do a simple animation, first, with the default cube. Figure 5-26 to Figure 5-39 shows the step-by-step procedure.

After you open Blender, go to the Animation workspace. By default, the toolbar isn't open in the 3D Viewport, so press T on the keyboard to show it, and click the Move tool (see Figure 5-26).

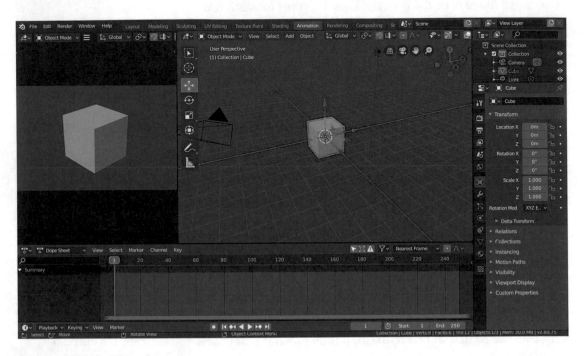

Figure 5-26. *First Step*

Move the cube and assign a keyframe by pressing I while your cursor is in the 3D Viewport, and then click Location. Repeat the action, but this time, click Rotation (see Figure 5-27).

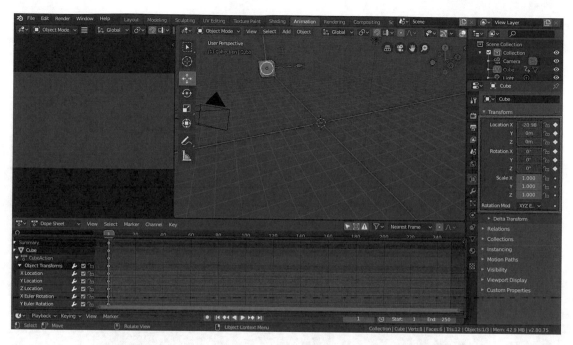

Figure 5-27. *Second step*

In the Dope Sheet Editor, you see small orange circles. This is the keyframe. You might wonder why it was in circle. When you view it in Timeline, you will see it in diamond like what you can see in Figure 5-28. You can also see in the Properties, in the Transform panel that beside the Location and Rotation value there is a diamond shape, and the rectangle where the value is dark yellow. This means that this part has a keyframe.

Figure 5-28. *The view in Timeline*

Now add a keyframe in the material. Click the Base Color and press I in the keyboard. Do the same in the Subsurface color. In Figure 5-29, a dark yellow color outlines the rectangle for the Base color and Subsurface color values. This means that it already has a keyframe. In Figure 5-29, Dope Sheet, Material ➤ Shader Nodetree holds the keyframe for the material.

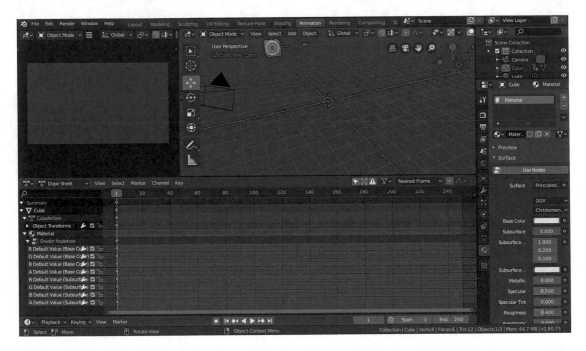

Figure 5-29. *Third Step*

Now move the playhead (the blue vertical line) in the Dope Sheet, and you will see that the playhead of the Timeline moves too. The color of the location and rotation changes from orange to green in Figure 5-30. Green means that there is no keyframe **but** it was already part of the animation.

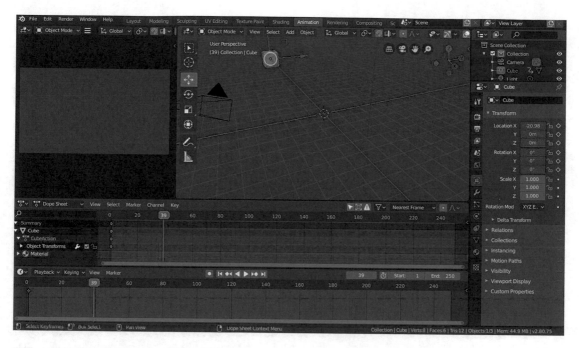

Figure 5-30. *Moving on the Frame*

Take a look at the Location color. As you move the cube, the location color changes to orange (see Figure 5-31). This means it isn't keyframed and it isn't part of the animation. Unless you put a keyframe on it, the previous value is the one considered.

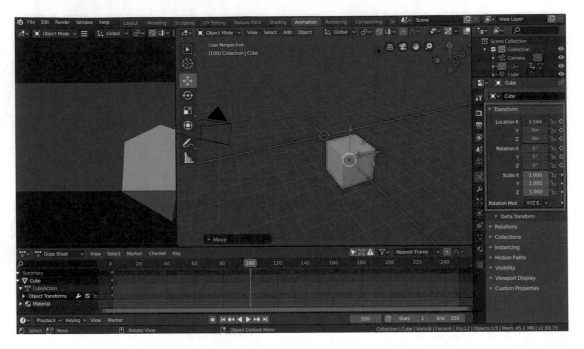

Figure 5-31. *Moving the Object*

Make sure to move the cube in the x axis and change its rotation. Also change the Material settings. Again, put at keyframe on it by pressing I on the keyboard and clicking Location for location and Rotation for rotation. For materials, press the I key after clicking the Base color and the Subsurface color (see Figure 5-32).

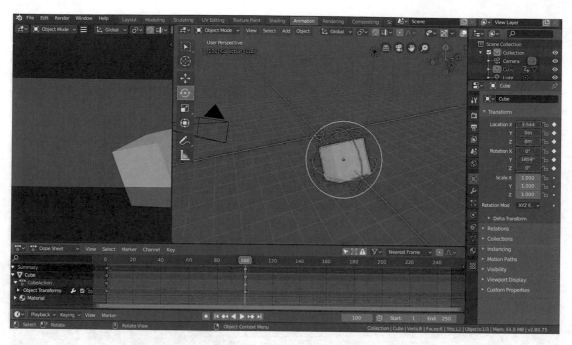

Figure 5-32. *Fourth Step*

Let's see how it looks (see Figure 5-33).

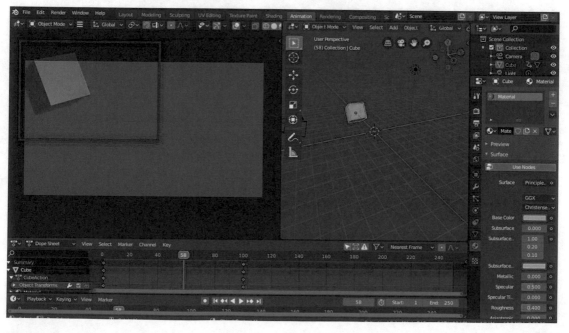

Figure 5-33. *Rendered view in 3D*

Observe the changes happened in the cube by looking at Figure 5-34.

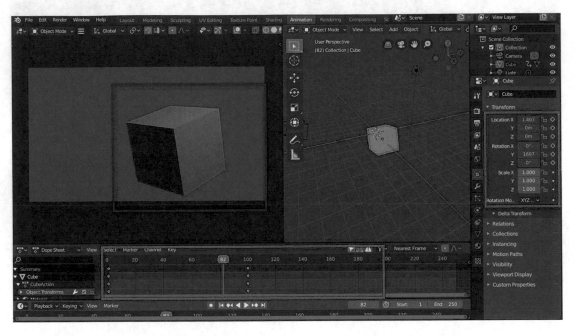

Figure 5-34. *Rendered with 3D Viewport*

As you can see, when we don't have keyframes in between, the animation continues. When the playhead is in between, the color of the Location value, Rotation value, Base color value, and Subsurface value is in green, which represents animation from the first keyframe to the second keyframe.

Figure 5-35 shows the Dope Sheet when you add an interpolation mode. Even though I want to show you the effect of each interpolation mode, it's hard to do it with screenshots, but you can check out a sample at `http://robertpenner.com/easing/`.

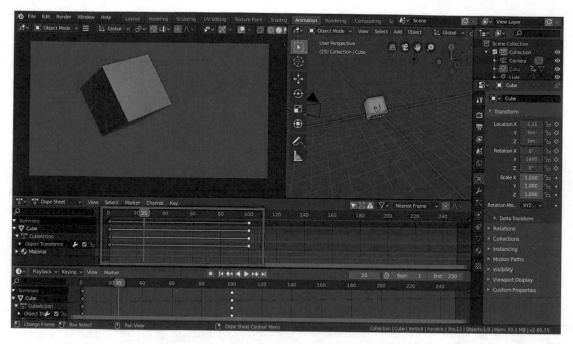

Figure 5-35. *Interpolation mode*

Figure 5-36 shows how it looks in the Graph Editor. The small dot that you can see along the line is what represents the handle. When you move it, it affects the animation you've created for your project so better to understand this much. Every line represents every action. For example, there is a line represents your move in x axis, another line for y axis, another line for Z-axis and there is a different set for rotation and materials so you need to understand this before editing this one.

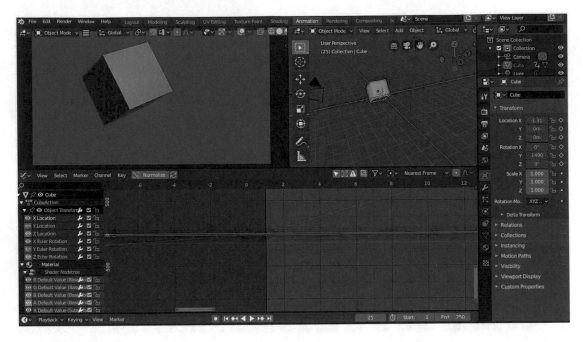

Figure 5-36. *Graph Editor*

Figure 5-37 shows how it looks in the Action Editor. As you can see, it shows simple data. It doesn't show anything related to the materials.

The name is CubeAction. You can rename it in the rectangle by clicking it and when you see your cursor in it, rename it the way you want. As we create an action, Blender automatically creates a name for it.

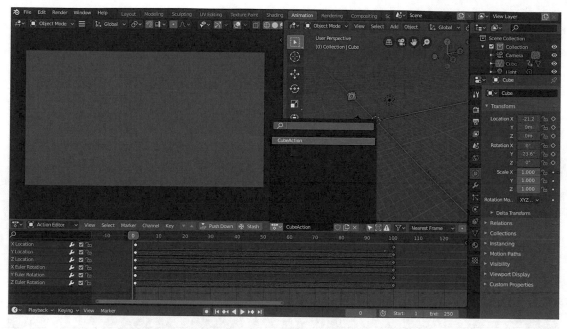

Figure 5-37. *Action Editor*

In Figure 5-38, we don't have any data in these three editors. The Shape Key Editor is only for shape keys, and we don't have any present.

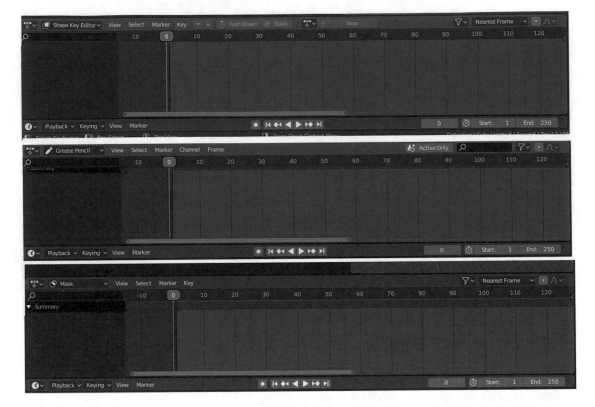

Figure 5-38. *Shape Key Editor, Grease Pencil and Mask*

What is Shape Keys? Shape keys support different target shapes (such as facial expressions) to be controlled. This deforms objects into new shapes for animation. In other terminology, shape keys may be called morph targets or blend shapes. This is helpful in character animation and the likes.

Mask mode doesn't have any data in it because we don't have anything that is in mask. Grease Pencil mode creates 2D animation.

Rendering Workspace

Rendering is the process of turning a 3D scene into a 2D image. As you know, Blender includes three render Engines with different strengths. Eevee is a physically based real-time renderer. Cycles is a physically based path tracer. Workbench is designed for layout, modeling, and previews.

What the render looks like is defined by cameras, lights, and materials. These are shared between Eevee and Cycles; however, some features are only supported in one or the other.

Renders can be split up into layers and passes, which can then be composited together for creative control or to combine layers with real footage. Freestyle can add non-photorealistic line rendering.

Blender supports interactive 3D Viewport rendering for all render engines, for quick integration of lighting and shading. Once this is done, the final quality image or animation can be rendered and output to disk.

Figure 5-39 shows the setup of this workspace.

Figure 5-39. *Rendering workspace. (Image Editor: green; Properties: yellow; and Timeline: red)*

The Image Editor differs from the Image Editor in the Shading workspace. Let's discuss the Image Editor in the Rendering workspace.

First, when you want to render your project, for you shows the product, you need first to go to Render menu ➤ Render Image or press F12 if rendering image or Render menu ➤ Render Animation or hold Ctrl+F12 for rendering animation. Then you will see a new window opened, as shown in Figure 5-40.

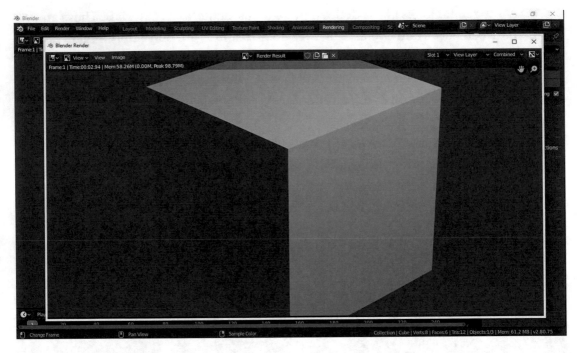

Figure 5-40. *Rendered image*

As you can see in Figure 5-40, when you rendered an image/animation, another window is being opened and behind it is the main window of Blender.

Unless you rendered an image, most of the command in the Rendering workspace will continue to be disabled. After you close this window, the rendered image is shown in the Image Editor slot that you can see in the Rendering workspace, like in Figure 5-41.

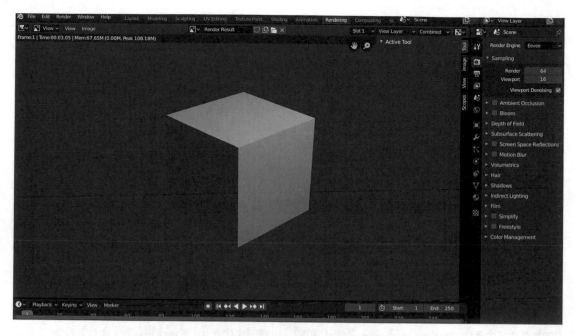

Figure 5-41. *Rendered image in the Rendering workspace*

Now, let's see the difference between the Image Editor of Shading workspace and the Rendering workspace. Figure 5-42 for the shading workspace and Figure 5-43 for the Rendering workspace to start comparing the Image Editor.

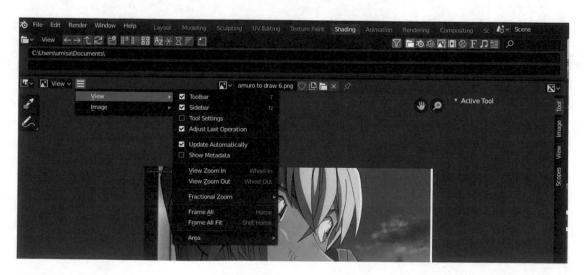

Figure 5-42. *Image Editor in the Shading workspace*

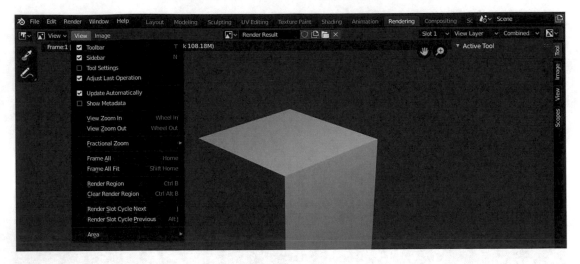

Figure 5-43. *Image Editor in Rendering workspace*

They both have the same tools in the toolbar: Sample and Annotate tools. They both have the three modes View, Paint, and Mask. In the Image Editor of rendering workspace, there is the Fake User button, New Image button, Open button, and Delete button; but it doesn't have the Image Pin button. They both have Tool, Image, View, and Scope panels. But as in the View menu, there are differences. There are commands in the Rendering workspace's Image Editor that isn't available in the Image Editor.

Header Menus

Let's first talk about the Header menus (see Figure 5-44).

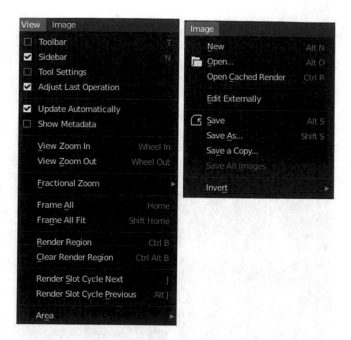

Figure 5-44. *View menu and Image menu of Image Editor in Rendering workspace*

Again, the View menu is pretty self-explanatory.

The two interesting options from the Image menu are: **Open Cached Render** (Ctrl+R) reads all the current scene's view layers from cache as needed. **Edit Externally** edits image in an eternal application.

Let's talk about the panels on the right side of the Image Editor, as seen in Figure 5-45.

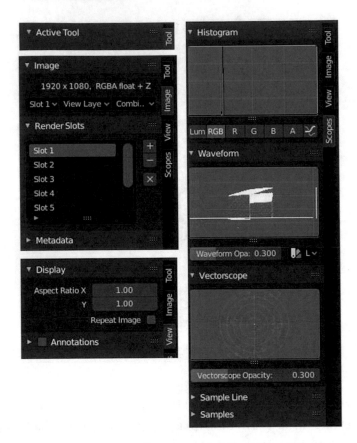

Figure 5-45. *Tool, Image, View and Scope panel*

These panels are almost the same as the Shading workspace's Image Editor. What is different are Source, Color Space, Alpha, Image Path, a checkbox for View as Render and metadata. Here you see render slots.

Render slots are slots available for your rendered image. That slot is the huge space provided in the Image Editor, where you can see the rendered image. By default, the first image is placed in Slot1. If you choose the slot2, you will see nothing unless you rendered again on that slot. You can do that by choosing the slot number in the Select menu of the slots in the Header region, as you can see in Figure 5-46.

Figure 5-46. *Slot select menu*

If you didn't change your slot here, click the render image; whatever rendered image was placed in the slot is replaced by the new rendered image.

Sample Project

This sample project shows the differences between the three render engine's output. Figure 5-47 is the result of the Workbench render.

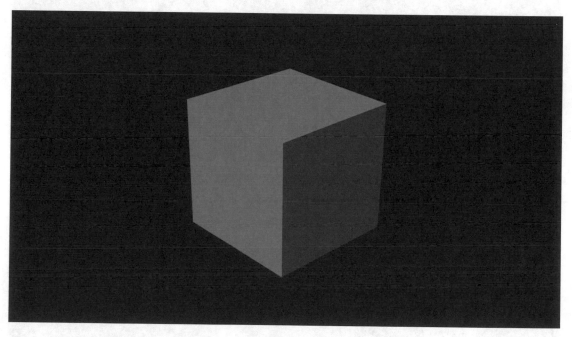

Figure 5-47. *Workbench Rendered result*

Figure 5-48 is the result of the Eevee render.

Figure 5-48. *Eevee rendered result*

Figure 5-49 is the result of the Cycles render.

Figure 5-49. *Cycles Rendered result*

Workbench's differences can easily be noticed with this default cube because of its lighting. Eevee and Cycles differ but they are hard to distinguish because at first glance of this simple project, they are similar. Actually, Cycles is more detailed than Eevee and the shadows in Cycles are darker if you look at it closely.

A complex project can make you learn differences: character modeling uses hair particles, architectural visualization uses different kinds of lighting, and so forth.

Camera Fundamentals

The camera is one of the most important parts in rendering a scene.

Capturing an ideal shot isn't that simple. There are a lot of things to consider but I'll give you some of the basic things so that you can apply when rendering an image.

First is the **Aperture**. This refers to the diameter of the hole inside the lens. A change in aperture alters the size of this hole, allowing more or less light into the camera, which also has an effect on the depth of field of your final image. You can image this as something like a pupil of your eye. The wider the aperture, the more light is allowed in.

Second, there is the **Shutter Speed**. The mirror flips up and the shutter opens, recording the light present onto the sensor. The speed at which this happens determines the exposure length as well as the amount of motion blur. After the light passes the aperture, it then reaches the shutter.

Third, there is the **ISO.** The sensor captures the light and is controlled by the ISO. The higher you set, the more sensitive it is, but it'll also capture more digital noise. Once the light passes the Aperture and been filtered by the shutter speed, it reaches the sensor. This is where the ISO comes in. As you turn the ISO number up, you increase the exposure but at the same time, the quality of the image decreases.

I'll stop with these basic camera fundamentals. You can learn more at `http://expertphotography.com`.

I left out three things in the Properties section in Chapter 2: Objects Constraints, Particles, and Physics. Let's talk about them now.

Note   There's no sample project for Object Constraints, Particles and Physics because I don't think it is easy to demonstrate it with figures so our discussion for these three is a thorough tour to give you an idea what's available in Blender. The rest is up to your imagination.

Object Constraints

Constraints are a way to control an object's properties, for example its location, rotation or scale, using either plain static value or another object called target.

Figure 5-50 shows the list of Object Constraints in Mesh.

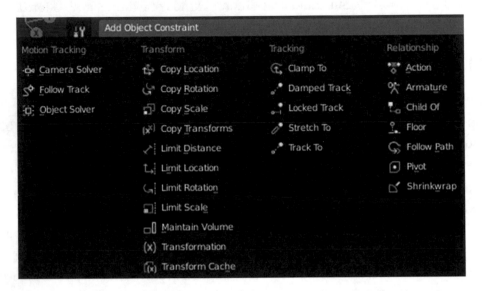

Figure 5-50. *Object Constraints*

Even though constraints are useful in static projects, their main usage is in animation.

- You can control an object's animation through the targets used by its constraints. Indeed, these targets can then control the constraint's owner's properties, and hence, animating the targets will indirectly animate the owner.

- You can animate constraints' settings.

Constraints in Blender work with Objects and Bones. Constraints work in combination with each other to form a Constraint Stack.

Constraints are a fantastic way to add sophistication and complexity to a rig but be careful not to rush in too quickly, piling up constraints until you lose all sense of how they interact with each other.

Constraints are divided into four categories: Motion Tracking, Transform, Tracking, and Relationship.

Motion Tracking Constraints

Let's discuss the constraints under Motion Tracking: Camera Solver, Follow Track, and Object Solver.

Camera Solver Constraint gives the owner (object) of the constraints the location and rotation of the solved camera motion. The solved camera motion is where the Blender reconstructs the position of the physical, real-world camera, when it filmed the video footage, relative to the thing being tracked. This constraints only works after you have set up a minimum of eight markers and clicked Solved Camera Motion in Movie Clip Editor ➤ Toolbar ➤ Solve ➤ Solve Camera Motion.

Figure 5-51 shows its settings.

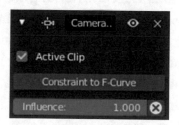

Figure 5-51. *Camera Solver Constraint settings*

Active Clip makes the constraints receive tracking data from the Movie Clip Editor but an option appears to choose from other clips. **Constraints to F-Curve** applies the constraint creating Keyframes for the transform. **Influence** is the amount of constraint on the final solution.

Follow Track Constraint makes objects have the same position at a frame as the track has and the motion of this object happens on a single plane defined by the camera and the original position of the object.

Figure 5-52 shows its settings.

Figure 5-52. *Follow Track Constraint*

Active Clip makes the constraints receive tracking data from the Movie Clip Editor but an option appears to choose from other clips. **3D position** uses the 3D position of the track to the parent. **Undistort** parents to the undistorted position of the 2D track. **Frame Method** defines how the footage is fitted in the camera frame. **Camera** selects the camera to which the motion is parented to, and if active, an empty scene camera is used. **Depth Object** constraint objects are projected onto the surface of this depth object, which can create facial makeup visual effects when this field is set. **Constraint to F-curve** creates F-curve for the objects that copies the movement cause by the constraints. **Influence** is the amount of constraint on the final solution.

Object Solver Constraint gives the owner of this constraint, the location, and rotation of the Solved Object Motion.

Note   Don't be confused, okay? Camera Solver Constraint is for Solved Camera Motion. Object Solver Constraint is of Solved Object Motion. Camera ➤ Camera, Object ➤ Object.

The Solved Object Motion is where Blender thinks the physical, real-world (tracked) object was, relative to the camera that filmed it. This constraint only works after you have set up a minimum of eight markers and clicked Solved Object Motion in Movie Clip Editor ➤ Toolbar ➤ Solve ➤ Solve Camera Motion or Movie Clip Editor ➤ Sidebar region ➤ Objects.

Figure 5-53 shows its settings.

Figure 5-53. *Object Solver Constraint*

Active Clip makes the constraints receive tracking data from the Movie Clip Editor but an option appears to choose from other clips. **Object** selects a tracked object to receive transform data from. **Camera** selects the camera to which the motion is parented to and if active empty scene camera is used. **Set Inverse** moves the origin of the object to the origin of the camera. **Clear Inverse** moves the origin of the object back to the spot set in the Movie Clip Editor. **Constraints to F-curve** applies the constraint creating keyframes for the transform. **Influence** is the amount of constraint on the final solution.

Transform Constraints

Let's proceed to the constraints under Transform: Copy Location, Copy Rotation, Copy Scale, Copy Transforms, Limit Distance, Limit Location, Limit Rotation, Limit Scale, Maintain Volume, Transformation, and Transform Cache.

Copy Location Constraint forces its owner to have the same location as its target. Figure 5-54 shows its settings.

Figure 5-54. *Copy Location Constraint*

Target is the data ID selects the constraints target and is not functional (red state) when it is none. **XYZ** controls the axes that are constrained. **Invert** inverts their respective preceding coordinates. **Offset** allows the owner to be moved using its current transform properties relative to its target's position. **Space** is the standard conversion between spaces. **Influence** is the amount of constraint on the final solution.

I'd like to note that the meaning when the name of your constraint or eve modifier becomes red as you add it like in Figure 5-55, it means there's an error while you're adding it. Like it isn't applicable in the object where you add it. In this case, the reason why the constraint is in a red state is because the Target is not yet set.

Copy Rotation Constraint forces its owner to match rotation of its target.

Figure 5-55 shows its settings.

Figure 5-55. *Copy Location Constraint*

Target is the data ID selects the constraints target and is not functional (red state) when it is none. **XYZ** controls the axes that are constrained. **Invert** inverts their respective rotation values. **Offset** allows the owner to be rotated relative to its target's orientation. **Space** is standards conversion between spaces. **Influence** is the amount of constraint on the final solution.

Copy Scale Constraint forces its owner to have the same scale as its target.

Figure 5-56 shows its settings.

Figure 5-56. *Copy Scale Constraint*

Target is the data ID selects the constraints target and is not functional (red state) when it is none. **XYZ** controls along which axes the scale is constrained. **Power** allows raising the copied scale to the specified arbitrary power. **Offset** the constraints combines the copied scale with the owner's scale instead of overwriting it. **Additive** uses addition instead of multiplication in the implementation of the Offset option. **Space** means standards conversion between spaces. **Influence** is the amount of constraint on the final solution.

Copy Transforms Constraint forces its owner to have the same transforms as its target.

Figure 5-57 shows its settings.

Figure 5-57. *Copy Transforms Constraint*

Target is the data ID selects the constraints target and is not functional (red state) when it is none. **Space** means standards conversion between spaces. **Influence** is the amount of constraint on the final solution.

Limit Distance Constraint forces its owner to stay either further from, nearer to, or exactly at a given distance from its target. In other words, the owner's location is constrained outside, inside, or at the surface of a sphere centered on its target. When you specify a new target, the Distance value is automatically set to correspond to the distance between the owner and this target.

Figure 5-58 shows its settings.

Figure 5-58. *Limit Distance Constraint*

Target is the data ID selects the constraints target and is not functional (red state) when it is none. **Distance** sets the limit distance. **Reset Distance** resets distance value when clicked so that it corresponds to the actual distance between the owner and its target. **Clamp Region** allows you to choose how to use sphere defined by the Distance setting and target's origin. There are three options. Inside owner is constrained inside the sphere. Outside owner is constrained outside the owner. **Surface owner** is constrained on the surface of the sphere. **For Transform** restricts the resulting transform property values. **Space** means standards conversion between spaces. **Influence** is the amount of constraint on the final solution.

Limit Location Constraint restricts the amount of allowed translations along each axis, through lower and upper bounds.

Figure 5-59 shows its settings.

Figure 5-59. *Limit Location Constraint*

Mini XYZ enables the lower boundary for the location of the owner's origin along the x, y, and z axes of the chosen space. **The Mini XYZ number field** controls the value of Minimum limit. **Maxi XYZ** enables the upper boundary for the location of the owner's origin along respectively the X Y and Z axes of the chosen Space. The **Maxi XYZ number field** controls the value of Maximum limit. **For Transform** the owner's transform properties are limited by the constraint because the owner can still have coordinates out of bounds. **Convert** allows you to choose in which space to evaluate its owner's transform properties. **Influence** is the amount of constraint on the final solution.

Limit Rotation Constraint restricts the amount of allowed rotations around each axis, through lower and upper bounds.

Figure 5-60 shows its settings.

Figure 5-60. *Limit Rotation Constraint*

Limit XYZ enables the rotation limit around respectively the X, Y and Z axes of the owner, in the chosen Space. **Min/Max number fields** control the value of their lower and upper boundaries. **For Transform** the owner's transform properties are limited by the constraint because the owner can still have coordinates out of bounds. **Convert** allows you to choose in which space to evaluate its owner's transform properties. **Influence** is the amount of constraint on the final solution.

Limit Scale Constraint restricts the amount of allowed scaling along each axis, through lower and upper bounds. This constraint does not tolerate negative scale values when you add it to an object or bone, even if no axis limit is enabled. With the **For Transform** button, as soon as you scale your object, all negative scale values are instantaneously inverted to positive ones and the boundary settings can only take strictly positive values.

Figure 5-61 shows its settings.

Figure 5-61. *Limit Scale Constraint*

Mini XYZ enables the lower boundary for the scale of the owner along, respectively, the X, Y and Z axes of the chosen Space. **The Mini XYZ** number field controls the value of Minimum limit. **Maxi XYZ** enables the upper boundary for the scale of the owner along, respectively, the X, Y and Z axes of the chosen Space. The **Maxi XYZ** number field controls the value of Maximum limit. With **For Transform**, the owner's transform properties are limited by the constraint because the owner can still have coordinates that are out of bounds. **Convert** allows you to choose in which space to evaluate its owner's transform properties. **Influence** is the amount of constraint on the final solution.

Maintain Volume Constraint limits the volume of a mesh or a bone to a given ratio of its original volume.

Figure 5-62 shows its settings.

Figure 5-62. *Maintain Volume Constraint*

Mode specifies how the constraint handles scaling of the non-free axes. There are three options. **Strict** overrides non-free axis scaling to strictly maintain the specified volume. **Uniform** maintains the volume as specified only when the pre-constraint scaling is uniform. **Single Axis** maintains the volume only when the object is scaled on its free axis. **Free** free-scaling axis of the object. **Volume** sets the bone's rest volume. **Convert** allows you to choose which space to evaluate its owner's transform properties. **Influence** is the amount of constraint on the final solution.

Transformation Constraint is more complex and versatile than the other transform constraints. It allows you to map one type of transform properties of the target, to the same or another type of transform properties of the owner, within a given range of values. You can also switch between axes and use the range values not as limits, but rather as markers to define a mapping between input (target) and output (owner) values.

Figure 5-63 shows its settings.

Figure 5-63. *Transformation Constraint*

Target is the data ID selects the constraints target and is not functional (red state) when it is none. **Extrapolate**'s min and max values bound the input and output values. all values outside these ranges are clipped to them. When you enable this button, the min and max values are no longer strict limits but rather markers defining a proportional (linear) mapping between input and corresponding output values. **Source** contains the input (from target) settings. **Destination** contains the output (to owner) settings. **Space**

means standard conversion between spaces. **Influence** is the amount of constraint on the final solution.

Transform Cache Constraint streams animations made at the transformation matrix level.

Figure 5-64 shows its settings.

Figure 5-64. *Transform Cache Constraint*

The **Cache File** data-block menu selects the Alembic file. **File Path** is the path to the Alembic file. **Is Sequence** (when file is opened) **determines** whether the cache file is separated in a series of files. **Override Frame** (when file is opened) is an option to use a custom frame for looking up data in the cache file instead of using the current scene frame. **Manual Transform Scale** (when file is opened) **is the** value by which to enlarge or shrink the object with respect to the world's origin. **Object Path** (when file is opened) is the path to the Alembic object inside the archive. **Vertices/Faces/UV/Color** (when file is opened) **determines the** type of data to read for a mesh object, respectively. **Influence** is the amount of constraint on the final solution.

Tracking Constraints

Let's proceed to the constraints under the Tracking category: Clamp To, Damped Track, Locked Track, Stretch To, and Track To.

Clamp To Constraint clamps an object to a curve. It is very similar to the Follow Path constraint, but instead of using the evaluation time of the target curve, Clamp To will get the actual location properties of its owner (those shown in the Transform panel), and judge where to put it by mapping this location along the target curve.

Figure 5-65 shows its settings.

Figure 5-65. *Clamp To Constraint*

Target is the data ID to select the constraints target and is not functional (red state) when it is none. **Main** controls which global axis is the main direction of the path. **Cyclic** as soon as the object reaches one end of the curve it is instantaneously moved to its other end. **Influence** is the amount of constraint on the final solution.

Damped Track Constraint constrains one local axis of the owner to always point towards Target.

Figure 5-66 shows its settings.

Figure 5-66. *Damped Track Constraint*

Target is the data ID selects the constraints target and is not functional (red state) when it is none. **To** is the axis of the object you want to point at the Target object. **Influence** is the amount of constraint on the final solution.

Locked Track Constraint is a Track To constraint, but with a locked axis. Hence, the owner can only track its target by rotating around this axis, and unless the target is in the plane perpendicular to the locked axis, and crossing the owner, this owner cannot really point at its target.

Figure 5-67 shows its settings.

Figure 5-67. *Locked Track Constraint*

Target is the data ID selects the constraints target and is not functional (red state) when it is none. **To is** the tracking local axis. **Lock is** the locked local axis. **Influence** is the amount of constraint on the final solution.

Stretch To Constraint causes its owner to rotate and scale its y axis toward its target. So it has the same tracking behavior as the Track To constraint. However, it assumes that the y axis is the tracking and stretching axis, and does not give you the option of using a different one.

Figure 5-68 shows its settings.

Figure 5-68. *Stretch To Constraint*

Target is the data ID selects the constraints target and is not functional (red state) when it is none. **Rest Length** sets the rest distance between the owner and its target. **Reset** recalculates the Rest Length value so that it corresponds to the actual distance between the owner and its target. **Volume Variation** controls the amount of volume variation exponentially to the stretching amount. **Volume Min/Volume Max** limits for the volume preservation to a minimum and maximum scaling each by a Bulge factor.

Smooth is the smoothness factor to make limits less visible. **Volume** controls which of the x and/or z axes should be affected (scaled up/down) to preserve the virtual volume while stretching along the y axis. **Plane** controls which of the x or z axes should be maintained aligned with the global z axis, while tracking the target with the y axis. **Influence** is the amount of constraint on the final solution.

Track To Constraint applies rotations to its owner, so that it always points a given To axis towards its target, with another Up axis permanently maintained as much aligned with the global z axis (by default) as possible.

Figure 5-69 shows its settings.

Figure 5-69. *Track To Constraint*

Target is the data ID selects the constraints target and is not functional (red state) when it is none. **To** the tracking local axis. **Up** is the upward most local axis. When **Target-Z** means the Up axis is aligned with the target's local z axis. **Space** is the standard conversion between spaces. **Influence** is the amount of constraint on the final solution.

Relationship Constraints

Let's discuss the Relationship category, which includes Action, Armature, Child Of, Floor, Follow Path, Pivot, and Shrinkwrap.

Action Constraint allows you control an action using the transformations of another object.

Figure 5-70 shows its settings.

Figure 5-70. *Action Constraint*

Target is the data ID selects the constraints target and is not functional (red state) when it is none. **Bone** you can use this field when the target is an armature object. **Transform Channel** controls which transform property (location rotation or scale along/around one of its axes) from the target to use as action driver. **Target Space** allows you to choose the space to evaluate its target's transform properties. **To Action** selects the name of the action you want to use. **Object Action** this option makes the constrained bone use the object part of the linked action instead of the same-named pose part. This allows you to apply the action of an object to a bone. **Target Range Min/Max** lower and upper bounds of the driving transform property value. **Action Range Start/End** starting and ending frames of the action to be mapped. **Influence** is the amount of constraint on the final solution.

Armature Constraint is the constraint version of the Armature Modifier, exactly reproducing the weight-blended bone transformations and applying it to its owner orientation. It can be used like a variant of the Child Of constraint that can handle multiple parents at once, but requires all of them to be bones.

Figure 5-71 shows its settings.

Figure 5-71. *Armature Constraint*

Add Target Bone adds a new empty entry at the end of the target list. **Normalize Weights** normalizes all weight values in the target list so that they add up to 1.0. **Preserve Volume** enables the use of quaternions for preserving the volume of the object during deformation. **Use Envelopes** to approximate envelope-only behavior of the modifier add all relevant bones with weight 1.0. **Influence** is the amount of constraint on the final solution.

Child Of Constraint is the constraint version of the standard parent/children relationship between objects.

Figure 5-72 shows its settings.

Figure 5-72. *Child Of Constraint*

Target the target object that this object will act as a child of. **Location XYZ** makes the parent affect or not affect the location along the corresponding axis. **Rotation XYZ** makes the parent affect or not affect the rotation around the corresponding axis. **Scale XYZ** makes the parent affect or not affect the scale along the corresponding axis. **Set inverse** restores the owner to its before-parenting state. **Clear Inverse** cancels the effect of set inverse and restores the owner/child to its default state regarding its target/parent. **Influence** is the amount of constraint on the final solution.

Floor Constraint allows you to use its target position (and optionally rotation) to specify a plane with a forbidden side, where the owner cannot go.

Figure 5-73 shows its settings.

Figure 5-73. *Floor Constraint*

Targets is the data ID selects the constraints target and is not functional (red state) when it is none. **Use Rotation** forces the constraint to take the target's rotation into account and allows you to have a floor plane of any orientation you like. **Offset** allows you to offset the floor from the target's origin by the given number of units. **Max/Min** controls the plane that is the floor. **Space** means the standard conversion between spaces. **Influence** is the amount of constraint on the final solution.

Follow Path Constraint places its owner onto a curve target object, and makes it move along this curve (or path). It can also affect its owner's rotation to follow the curve's bends, when the Follow Curve option is enabled.

Figure 5-74 shows its settings.

Figure 5-74. *Follow Path Constraint*

Targets is the data ID selects the constraints target and is not functional (red state) when it is none. **Animate Path** adds an F-curve with options for the start and end frame. **Follow Curve** if it is not activated the owner's rotation is not modified by the curve but when activated its effect is based on the option you will select between this two: Forward axis of the object that has to be aligned with the forward direction of the path and the Up axis of the object that has to be aligned with the world z axis**. Curve Radius** concerns objects scaled by the curve radius. **Fixed Position** objects stay locked to a single point somewhere along the length of the curve regardless of time. **Offset** is the number of frames to offset from the animation defined by the path. **Influence** is the amount of constraint on the final solution.

Pivot Constraint allows the owner to rotate around a target object. It was originally intended for pivot joints found in humans e.g. fingers, feet, elbows, and so forth.

Figure 5-75 shows its settings.

Figure 5-75. *Pivot Constraint*

Target is the data ID for the selection of the object to be used as a pivot point. **Use relative Offset** enables usage of Relative offset. **Relative Pivot Point XYZ** offset of pivot from target. **Pivot when** sets when to use the pivot. There are seven options. **Always** uses the pivot point in every rotation. -**X Ro**t uses the pivot point in the negative rotation range around the x axis. -**Y Rot** uses the pivot point in the negative range around the y axis. -**Z Rot** uses the pivot point in the negative rotation range around the z axis. **X Rot** uses the pivot point in the positive rotation range in x axis. **Y Rot** uses the pivot point in the positive rotation range in y axis. **Z Rot** uses the pivot point in the positive rotation range in the z axis. **Influence** is the amount of constraint on the final solution.

Shrinkwrap Constraint is the object counterpart of the Shrinkwrap Modifier. It moves the owner origin and therefore the owner object's location to the surface of its target.

Figure 5-76 shows its settings.

Figure 5-76. *Shrinkwrap Constraint*

Target is the data ID selects the constraint's target, which must be a mesh object, and is not functional when it has none. **Distance** is number field controls the offset of the owner from the shrunk computed position on the target's surface. **Shrinkwrap type** allows you to select which method to use to compute the point on the target's surface to move the owner's origin. There are four options. **Nearest Surface Point** shrinks the location to the nearest target surface. **Project** shrinks the location to the nearest target surface along a given axis. **Nearest Vertex** shrinks the location to the nearest target vertex. **Target Normal Project** shrinks the location to the nearest target surface along the interpolated vertex normals of the target**.**

Snap mode allows you to choose a snapping mode for this constraint. There are five options. With **Surface**, the point is constrained to the surface of the target object with distance offset towards the original point location. Inside the point is constrained to be inside the target object. With **Outside**, the point is constrained to be outside the target object. With **Outside Surface**, the point is constrained to the surface of the target object with distance offset always to the outside towards or away from the original location. With **Above Surface**, the point is constrained to the surface of the target object with distance offset applied exactly along the target normal**. Align Axis to Normal** aligns the specified axis to the surface normal. **Influence** is the amount of constraint on the final solution.

Visit `https://docs.blender.org/manual/en/latest/animation/constraints/index.html` to learn more about Blender object constraints.

Particles

Particles are lots of items emitted from mesh objects, typically in the thousands. Each particle can be a point of light or a mesh, and be joined or dynamic. They may react to many different influences and forces, and have the notion of a lifespan. Dynamic particles can represent fire, smoke, mist, and other things such as dust or magic spells.

There are two types of particles: Hair and Emitter. In Hair, particles rendered as strands while in Emitter, particles are emitted in an object.

The following is Particle system workflow process.

1. Create the mesh that emits particles.

2. Create one or more Particle Systems to emit from the mesh. Many times, multiple particle systems interact or merge with each other to achieve the overall desired effect.

3. Tailor each Particle System's settings to achieve the desired effect.

4. Animate the base mesh and other particle meshes involved in the scene.

5. Define and shape the path and flow of the particles.

6. For Hair Particles Systems: Sculpt the emitter's flow (cut the hair to length and comb it)

7. Make the final render and do physics simulation, and tweak.

8. Bake your particles.

Figure 5-77 shows the Particle System settings in the Properties Editor.

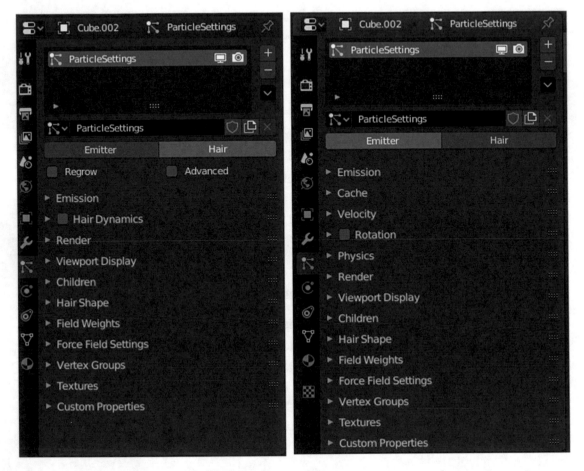

Figure 5-77. *Particle System in Properties Editor*

Let's briefly discuss each panel in each type of the Particle settings.

Emission Panel

Figure 5-78 shows the Emission panel.

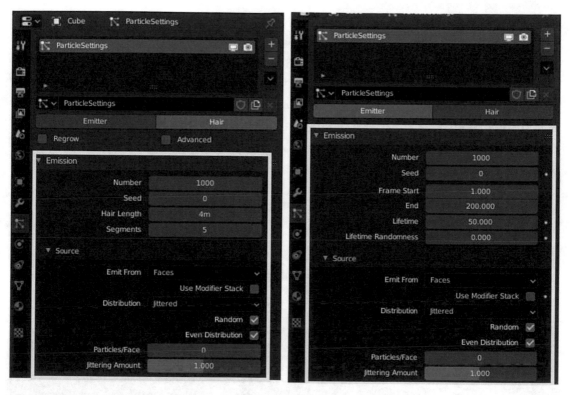

Figure 5-78. *Particle System ➤ Emission panel*

An Emitter system works like its name suggests; it emits/produces particles for a certain amount of time. In such a system, particles are emitted from the selected object from the Start frame to the End frame and have a certain lifespan. These particles are rendered as Halos, something you can see but they do not have any substance while Hair system, as its name suggested, can be used for strand-like objects, such as hair, fur, grass, quills and anything alike.

Let's analyze the emission panel between of Hair and Emitter base on Figure 5-78. Both of them have the **Number** setting is the maximum number of parent particles in the simulation. Both of them have the **Seed** settings, which is for offset in the random number table, to get a different randomized result. Both Hair and Emitter have the Source panel inside the Emission panel. The **Emit From** settings are where you indicate where to emit particles from. The **Distribution** settings are where you indicate how to distribute particles on selected element. The **Random** settings are where you enable the elements to emit in random order. The **Even Distribution** settings are where you use even distribution from faces based on face areas or edge length. The **Particles/Face** settings are where you indicate emission location. The **Jittering Amount** settings are where you indicate the amount of jitter applied to the sampling.

Let's talk about the differences. Hair particles have the **Hair Length** setting, where you can indicate the length of the hair strand. **Segments** settings, where you can indicate the number of hair segments. The Emitter particles have **Frame Start/End** settings, where you can indicate the frame number to start/end emitting particles. **Lifetime** settings, where you can indicate the life span of the particles. **Lifetime Randomness**, where you indicate the random variation of a particle life.

Cache Panel

By default, the Cache panel is visible in the Emitter tab, but in the Hair Particles tab, you need to enable the Hair Dynamics panel to show it.

Figure 5-79 shows the Cache panel.

Figure 5-79. *Particle System* ➤ *Cache panel*

They also have a lot of similar tools in this panel. They both have **Cache Step**, where you can indicate the number of frames between the cached frames. They also both have that long rectangle where you can see the list of cache, where you can rename it, add a cache, and delete one. They both can access to external location to read cache file by enabling the **External** setting. They also have **Bake/Calculate to Frame** button for bake physics, **Current Cache to Bake** button to bake the cache, **Bake All Dynamics/Update All to Frame** button, which is used for baking all physics. **Delete All Bakes** deletes all baked caches of all objects in the current scenes.

Hair particles have **Simulation start/end** settings, where you can indicate on which frame the simulation starts and ends.

Note   The simulation is only calculated for positive frames between the Start and End frames of the Cache panel, whether you bake or not. So if you want a simulation that is longer than the default frame range, you have to change the End frame. When animation is played, the physics writes each frame to the cache. For the cache to fill up, one has to start the playback before or on the frame that the simulation starts. The cache is cleared automatically on changes. But not on all changes, so it may be necessary to free it manually. The system is protected against changes after baking. If the mesh changes the simulation is not calculated as anew, the bake result can be cleared by clicking the Free Bake button on the simulation cache settings. A simulation can only be edited in Particle mode when it has been baked to a Disk Cache. If you are not allowed to write to the required subdirectory caching will not take place. Be careful with the sequence of modifiers in the modifier stack. You may have a different number of faces in the 3D Viewport and for rendering. If so, the rendered result may be very different from what you see in the 3D Viewport.

Hair Dynamics

Hair Dynamics is used for greater enhancement of hair particles or for animating hair particles.

Figure 5-80 shows this panel.

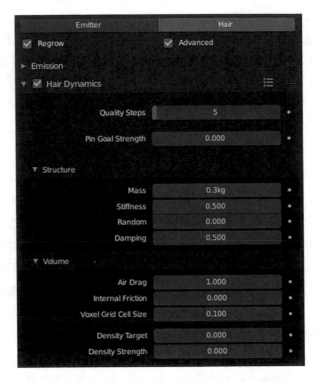

Figure 5-80. *Hair Particle System* ➤ *Hair Dynamics panel*

Quality Steps indicates the quality of the simulation in steps per frame. The **Pin Goal Strength** indicates pin spring stiffness. In Structure, **Mass** indicates the mass of cloth material. **Stiffness** indicates how much the material resists bending. **Random** indicates random stiffness in the hair. **Damping** indicates the amount of damping in bending behavior.

Air Drag indicates the thickness of the air that makes things falls slowly. **Internal friction** indicates the number of friction of hair volume. **Voxel Grid Cell Size** indicates the size of the voxel grid cells for interaction effects. **Density Target** indicates maximum hair density and **Density Strength** indicates the influence of target density on the simulation.

Note   A voxel represents a value on a regular grid in 3D space. Voxel grid is a 3D grid. A collection of aligned boxes.

Velocity Panel

When it comes to Hair Particles, Velocity panel, as well as Rotation and Physics, only appears when you check the Advanced option at the top of the Hair Particles settings.

Figure 5-81 shows this panel.

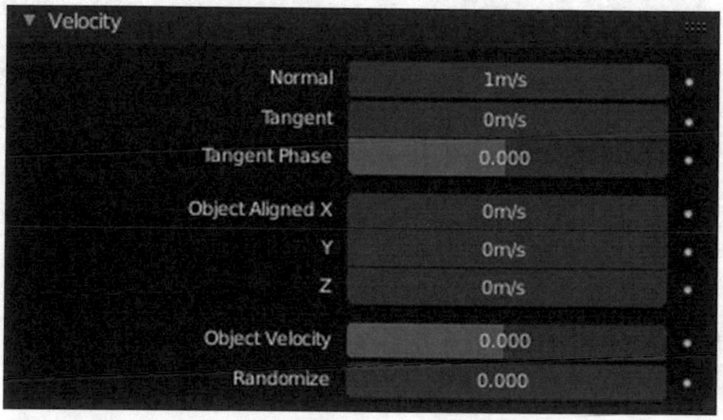

Figure 5-81. *Particle System ➤ Velocity panel*

When it comes to Hair Particles, Velocity panel, as well as Rotation and Physics, only appears when you check the Advanced option at the top of the Hair Particles settings.

Both Particles have the same settings for this panel. **Normal** lets the surface normal give the particle a starting velocity. **Tangent** lets the surface tangent give the particle a starting velocity. **Tangent Phase** rotates the surface tangent. **Object Aligned** lets the emitter object orientation give the particle a starting velocity. **Object Velocity** lets the object give the particle a starting velocity. **Randomize** gives the stating velocity a random variation.

Rotation Panel

Rotation panel have these tools: **Orientation Axis** sets the initial orientation of the particle. **Randomize** allows you to randomize particle orientation. **Phase** sets the rotation around the chosen axis. **Randomize Phase** where you can randomize the rotation around the chosen axis. The **Axis** settings allow you to choose which axis changes the particle rotation in time. The **Amount** settings are for the angular velocity amount. When the **Dynamic** tool in Emitter is enabled, the particles rotation is affected by collision and effectors.

Figure 5-82 shows the Rotation panel.

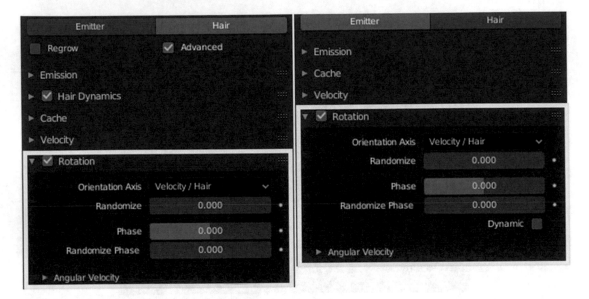

Figure 5-82. *Particle System ➤ Rotation panel*

Physics Panel

In this panel, both particles have the same settings. Figure 5-83 shows the panel.

Figure 5-83. *Particle System ➤ Physics panel*

Physics Type is where you can choose particles physics type. In Physics Type, there are five options: None, Newtonian, Keyed, Fluids, and Boids. **Mass** indicates the mass of the particles. **Forces** lets you see the settings of **Brownian**, where you can specify the amount of Brownian motion that adds random motion to the particles based on a Brownian noise field. **Brag** specifies the amount of force that reduces particles velocity in relation to its speed and size. **Damp** specifies the amount of reduces particle velocity.

Render Panel

Render As specifies how particles are rendered. There are four options for Hair Particles: None, Path, Object, and Collection. There are six options for Emitter: Collection, Object, Path, Line, Halo, and None. By default, Halo is set in Emitter while Path is set in Hair Particles. **Material** is a material slot for particle system. Both of them have **Coordinate System** specifies an object's coordinate system and **Path** sets **B-Spline** is for interpolation. **Steps** specifies the number of steps that paths are rendered with. **Timing** specifies the end time of drawn path through **End** settings, where you can give path length a random variation through **Random** settings.

Emitter Particles have two settings in the Render panel that are not available in Hair Particles. These are **Scale** where you can specify the size of the particles and **Scale Randomness** where you can give the particle size a random variation.

There are other functions, but I will not cover them.

Figure 5-84 shows this panel.

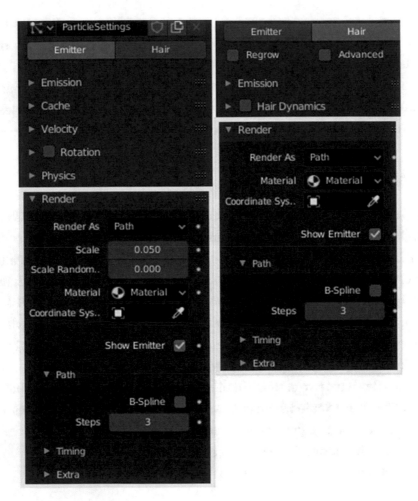

Figure 5-84. *Particle System ➤ Render panel*

Viewport Display Panel

Figure 5-85 shows the Viewport Display panel.

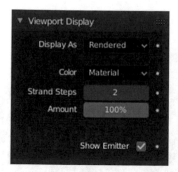

Figure 5-85. *Particle System* ➤ *Viewport Display panel*

For this panel, both particles have the same settings. **Display As** is where you choose how particles are drawn in viewport. There are six options on the Emitter tab: None, Rendered, Point, Circle, Cross, and Axis. There are three options on the Hair Particles tab: None, Rendered and Path. The default option set for both Emitter and Hair is Rendered. The **Color** setting is where you can choose where to draw additional particle data as color. There are four options: None, Material (default), Velocity, and Acceleration. **Strand Steps** is where you specify how many steps paths are drawn with while **Amount** is where you specify the percentage of particles to display in the 3D Viewport. Enabling **Show Emitter** makes the instancer visible in the viewport or the mesh that the particles are emitting from.

Children Panel

Figure 5-86 shows the Children panel.

Figure 5-86. *Particle System* ➤ *Children panel*

In this panel, both the Emitter and Hair particles have the same settings.

In this panel is where you can set the creation of child particles. As you can see in Figure 5-86, there are three options: None, Simple, and Interpolated. None means that no children are generated. Simple means that children are emitted from the parent position. Interpolated means that children are emitted between the Parents particles on the faces of a mesh. They interpolate between adjacent parents. This is especially useful for fur, because you can achieve an even distribution.

Hair Shape Panel

Figure 5-87 shows the Hair Shape panel.

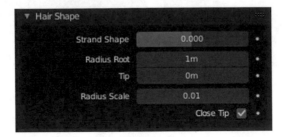

Figure 5-87. *Particle System ➤ Hair Shape panel*

This panel can be seen in both Emitter and Hair particles. **Strand Shape** specifies the strand shape parameter. **Radius Root** specifies the strand with at the root. **Tip** specifies the strand width at the tip. **Radius Scale** specifies the multiplier of radius properties. **Close Tip** sets the tip radius to 0.

Field Weights Panel

Figure 5-88 shows the Field Weights panel.

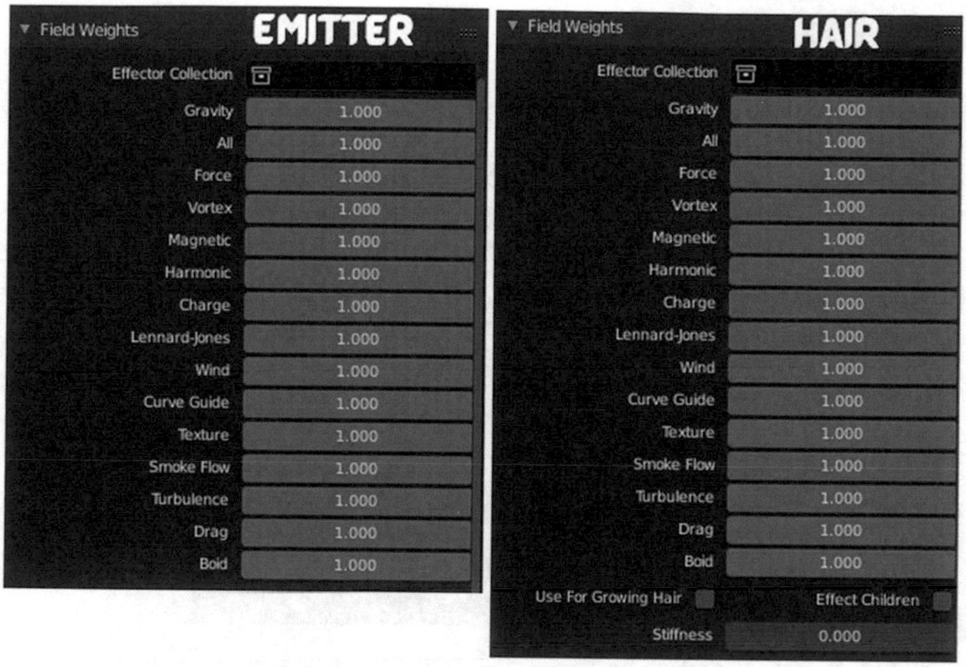

Figure 5-88. *Particle System ➤ Field Weights panel*

In this panel, the two particles settings have few differences. Let's talk first about the common settings.

Gravity specifies the global gravity weight. **All** specifies all effectors' weights. **Force** specifies the force effector weight. **Vortex** specifies the vortex effector weight. **Magnetic** specifies the magnetic effector weight. **Harmonic** specifies the harmonic effector weight. **Charge** specifies the charge effector weight. **Lennard-Jones** specifies the Lennard-Jones effector weight. **Wind** specifies the wind effector weight. **Curve Guide** specifies the Curve Guide effector weight. **Texture** specifies the texture effector weight. **Smoke Flow** specifies the Smoke Flow effector weight. **Turbulence** specifies the turbulence effector weight. **Drag** specifies the drag effector weight. **Boid** specifies the Boid effector weight.

In the Hair particle settings, **Stiffness** specifies the hair stiffness for effectors. **Use for Growing Hair** applies force fields when growing hair. **Effect Children** applies effectors to children.

Force Field Settings Panel

Figure 5-89 shows the Force Field Settings panel.

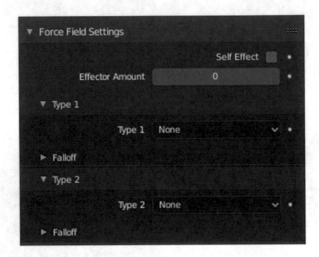

Figure 5-89. *Particle System ➤ Force Field Settings panel*

Both particles have the same settings in this panel. **Self Effect** makes particles effectors affect **Effector Amount**. **Type1** is the type of field. There are 14 options: Smoke Flow, Drag, Turbulence, Boid, Curve Guide, Texture, Lennard-Jones, Charge, Harmonic, Magnetic, Vortex, Wind, and Force. The settings that appear on **Falloff** depend on your choice in Type1. **Type2** has the same settings as Type1. This is for another option of field type.

Vertex Groups Panel

Figure 5-90 shows the Vertex Groups panel.

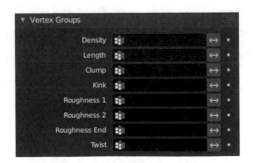

Figure 5-90. *Particle System ➤ Vertex Groups panel*

The panel's settings are the same for both particles.

Vertex Groups tag the vertices belonging to parts of a Mesh Objects or Lattice. Think of the legs of a chair or the hinges of a door, or hands, arms, limbs, head, feet, and so forth, of a character. In addition, you can assign different weight values to the vertices within a vertex group. Hence, vertex groups are sometimes also called weight groups.

Density controls the density. **Length** controls the length. **Clump** controls the clump. **Kink** controls the kink. **Roughness1/2** controls the roughness. **Roughness End** controls the roughness end. **Twist** controls the twist.

The arrow beside the rectangle is to negate the effect of the given effect to the vertex group; for example, the density.

Textures Panel

Textures are like additional layers on top of base material. Textures affect one or more aspects of the object's net coloring. The net color you see is a sort of layering effects.

Figure 5-91 shows the Textures panel.

Figure 5-91. Particle System ➤ Textures panel

Physics

Blender's Physics system allows you to simulate a number of different real-world physical phenomena. You can use these systems to create a variety of static and dynamic effects.

There are nine types of physics: Force Field, Collision, Cloth, Dynamic Paint, Soft Body, Fluid, Smoke, Rigid Body, and Rigid Body Constraint. Let's briefly discuss each.

Force Field Physics

Force Field offers a way to influence a simulation, in example to add extra movement. Particles, Soft Bodies, Rigid Bodies, and Cloth objects can all be affected by forces fields. Force fields automatically affect everything.

Its settings depend on which **Type** you choose. The Shape type sets the direction to calculate the effector force. There are 13 options available: Force (default), Wind, Vortex, Magnetic, Harmonic, Charge, Lennard-Jones, Texture, CurveGuide, Boid, Turbulence, Drag, and Smoke Flow.

There are types that have the same settings, and there are types that have only small differences.

Force Field Type ➤ Boid, Charge, Lennard-Jones, Magnetic, Wind Force, and Vortex

The settings for Boid, Charge, Lennard-Jones, Magnetic, and Wind are the same, but the application of these types is different. The settings of these five types have a lot of similarities to Force and Vortex settings too. So let's discuss its functions.

Boid is an artificial life program developed by Craig Reynolds in 1986. It simulates the flocking behavior of birds. The rules applied in the simplest Boids world are as follows.

Separation steers to avoid crowding local flock mates. Alignment: steer towards the average heading of local flock mates. **Cohesion** steers to move toward the average position of local flock mates. Complex rules can be added, such as obstacle avoidance and goal seeking.

Charge is similar to a *Force* type except it changes it's behavior based on the effected particles charge field, which means that this field has only an effect on particles that have also a Charge field.

Lennard-Jones is a very short range force with a behavior determined by the sizes of the effector and effected particles. At a distance smaller than the combined sizes, the field is very repulsive, but after that distance, it is attractive. It tries to keep the particles at an equilibrium distance from each other. Particles need to be at a close proximity to each other to be effected by this field at all.

Magnetic depends on the speed of the particles. It simulates the force of magnetism on magnetized objects.

Wind gives a constant force in a single direction, along the force object's local z axis. The strength of the force is visualized by the spacing of the circles.

Force is the simplest of the fields. It gives a constant force toward (positive strength) or away from (negative strength) the object's origin. Newtonian particles are attracted to a field with negative strength, and are blown away from a field with positive strength.

Vortex gives a spiraling force that twists the direction of points around the force object's local z axis. This can be useful for making a swirling sink, or a tornado, or kinks in particle hair.

Figure 5-92 shows the settings.

Figure 5-92. *Magnetic (represents the settings of Lennard-Jones, Wind, Charge, and Boid), Force, Vortex*

The following are under the Settings panel.

- **Shape**. Sets the direction to calculate the effector force.

    - **Point**. Points with omni-directional influence. Uses the object origin as the effector point.

    - **Line** (not part of Vortex Field). Field originates from the local z axis of the object.

    - **Plane**. Influences only in the local Z direction.

- **Surface** (not part of Vortex Field). The force fields act on a 3D object's surface. In this case, the z axis is the surface normal.

- **Every Point**. Uses every vertex in the mesh object as an effector point.

- **Surface Falloff**. Can only be found in the Vortex field.

- **Strength**. The strength of the force field.

- **Flow**. Convert effector force into air flow velocity.

- **Affect Location**. Affects particle location.

- **Affect Rotation**. Affects particle dynamic rotation.

- **Noise Amount**. The amount of noise for the force strength.

- **Seed**. Seed of the noise.

- **Gravitation** (Force Field only). Multiply force by 1/distance2.

- **Absorption**. Force is absorbed by collision objects.

The following are under the Falloff panel.

- **Shape**. Falloff type.

  - **Sphere**. The falloff is uniform in all directions.

  - **Tube**. The falloff results in a tube-shaped force field.

  - **Cone**. The falloff results in a cone-shaped force field.

- **Z Direction**. Effect in full or only positive/negative Z direction. There are three options for this one.

  - Both Z

  - Z+

  - Z-

- **Power**. How quickly strength falls off with distance from the force field.

- **Use minimum**. Use a minimum distance for the field's fall off.

- **Min Distance**. Minimum distance for the field's fall off.

- **Use maximum**. Use a maximum distance for the field to work.

Force Field Type ➤ Harmonic and Turbulence

These two have almost the same settings with each other. They only have a few differences.

In **Harmonic**, the source of the force field is the zero point of a harmonic oscillator. If you set the Damping parameter to 1, the movement is stopped in the moment the object is reached. This force field is really special if you assign it to particles.

Turbulence creates a random and chaotic 3D noise effect, similar to jets of water or geysers under the ocean.

Figure 5-93 shows its settings.

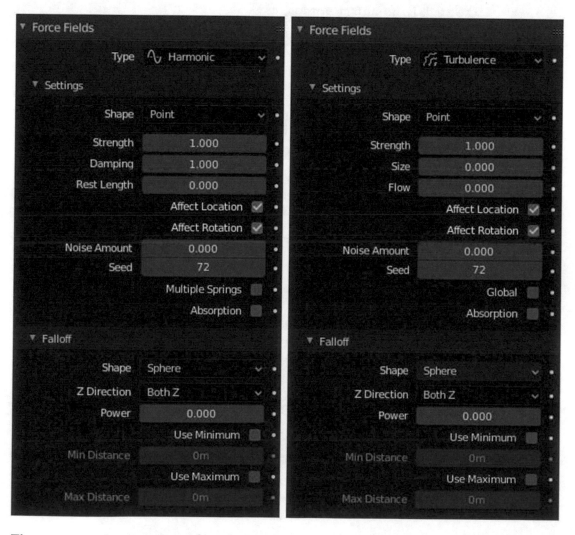

Figure 5-93. *Harmonic and Turbulence*

The following are under the Settings panel.

- **Shape**. Sets the direction that calculates the effector force.

  - **Point**. Point with omni-directional influence. Uses the object origin as the effector point.

  - **Line**. Field originates from the local z axis of the object.

  - **Plane**. Influence only in the local Z direction.

  - **Surface**. The force fields act on a 3D object's surface. In this case, the z axis is the surface normal.

  - **Every Point**. Uses every vertex in the mesh object as an effector point.

- **Strength**. The strength of the force field.

- **Flow**. Convert effector force into air flow velocity.

- **Damping (Harmonic)**. Damping of the harmonic force.

- **Rest Length (Harmonic)**. Rest length of the harmonic force.

- **Size (Turbulence)**. Size of the Turbulence.

- **Affect Location**. Affects particle location.

- **Affect Rotation**. Affects particle dynamic rotation.

- **Noise Amount**. The amount of noise for the force strength.

- **Seed**. Seed of the noise.

- **Multiple Springs (Harmonic)**. Every point is affected by multiple strings.

- **Global (Turbulence)**. Use effector/global coordinates for Turbulence.

- **Absorption**. Force is absorbed by collision objects.

The following are under the Falloff panel.

- **Shape**. Falloff type.

    - **Sphere**. The falloff is uniform in all directions.

    - **Tube**. The falloff results in a tube-shaped force field.

    - **Cone**. The falloff results in a cone-shaped force field.

- **Z Direction**. Effect in full or only positive/negative Z direction. There are three options for this one.

    - Both Z

    - Z+

    - Z-

- **Power**. How quickly strength falls off with distance from the force field.

- **Use minimum**. Use a minimum distance for the field's fall off.

- **Min Distance**. Minimum distance for the field's fall off.

- **Use maximum**. Use a maximum distance for the field to work.

Force Field Type ➤ Curve Guide

This forces particles to follow a certain path defined by a Curve Object. A typical scenario would be to move a red blood cell inside a vein, or to animate the particle flow in a motor. You can also use Curve Guide to shape certain hair strands.

Figure 5-94 shows its settings.

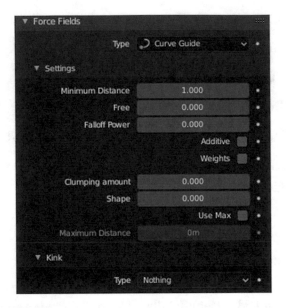

Figure 5-94. *Curve Guide*

The following are under the Settings panel.

- **Minimum Distance**. The distance from which particles are affected fully.

- **Free**. Guide-free time from particle life's end.

- **Falloff Power**. How quickly strength falls off with distance from the force field.

- **Additive**. Based on distance/falloff it adds a portion of the entire path.

- **Weights**. Use curve weights to influence the particle influence along the curve.

- **Clumping Amount**. The amount of clumping.

- **Shape**. Shape of clumping.

- **Use Max**. Use a minimum distance for the field to work.

- **Maximum Distance**. Maximum distance for the field to work.

The following are under the Kink panel.

- Type. The type of periodic offset on the curve. There are seven options for this kink: Roll, Rotation, Braid, Wave, Radial, Curl, and Nothing, which is the default value.

Force Field Type ➤ Drag

This force field type resists particle motion by slowing it down. Figure 5-95 shows its settings.

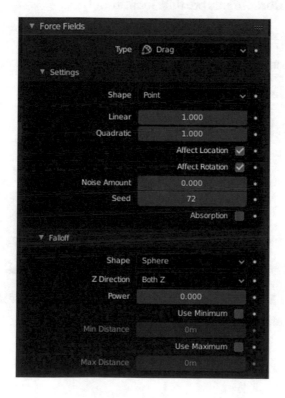

Figure 5-95. *Drag*

The following are under the Settings panel.

- **Shape**. Sets the direction to calculate the effector force.

  - **Point**. Point with omni-directional influence. Uses the object origin as the effector point.

  - **Line**. Field originates from the local z axis of the object.

- **Plane**. Influence only in the local Z direction.

- **Surface**. The force field acts on a 3D object's surface. In this case, the z axis is the surface normal.

- **Every Point**. Uses every vertex in the mesh object as an effector point.

- **Linear**. Drag component proportional to velocity.

- **Quadratic**. Drag component proportional to the square of velocity.

- **Affect Location**. Affects particle location.

- **Affect Rotation**. Affects particle dynamic rotation.

- **Noise Amount**. The amount of noise for the force strength.

- **Seed**. Seed of the noise.

- **Absorption**. Force is absorbed by collision objects.

The following are under the Falloff panel.

- **Shape**. Falloff type.

  - **Sphere**. The falloff is uniform in all directions.

  - **Tube**. The falloff results in a tube-shaped force field.

  - **Cone**. The falloff results in a cone-shaped force field.

- **Z Direction**. Effect in full or only positive/negative Z direction. There are three options for this one.

  - Both Z

  - Z+

  - Z-

- **Power**. How quickly strength falls off with distance from the force field.

- **Use minimum**. Use a minimum distance for the field's fall off.

- **Min Distance**. Minimum distance for the field's fall off.

- **Use maximum**. Use a maximum distance for the field to work.

Force Field Type ➤ Texture

You can use a Texture force field to create an arbitrarily complicated force field, which force in the three directions is color coded. Red is coding for the x axis, green for the y axis, and blue for the z axis (like the color of the coordinate axes in the 3D View).

Figure 5-96 shows its settings.

Figure 5-96. *Texture*

The following are under the Settings panel.

- **Texture mode**. How the texture effect is calculated. There are three options: RGB, Curl, and Gradient.

- **Strength**. The strength of the force field.

- **Nabla**. Defines size of derivative offset used for calculating gradient and curl.

- **Use Coordinates**. Use object/global coordinates for texture.

- **2D**. apply force only in 2D.

The following are under the Texture panel.

- **Checkered icon** drop-down button. Browse texture to be linked.
- **New** button. Add new texture.

The following are under the Falloff panel.

- **Shape**. Falloff type.
  - **Sphere**. The falloff is uniform in all directions.
  - **Tube**. The falloff results in a tube-shaped force field.
  - **Cone**. The falloff results in a cone-shaped force field.
- **Z Direction**. Effect in full or only positive/negative Z direction. There are three options for this one.
  - Both Z
  - Z+
  - Z-
- **Power**. How quickly strength falls off with distance from the force field.
- **Use minimum**. Use a minimum distance for the field's fall off.
- **Min Distance**. Minimum distance for the field's fall off.
- **Use maximum**. Use a maximum distance for the field to work.

Force Field Type ➤ Smoke Flow

This force field type creates a force based on a Smoke simulation air flow. It applies the smoke simulation air flow velocity as a force to other simulations that use force fields.

Figure 5-97 shows its settings.

Figure 5-97. *Smoke Flow*

The following are under the Settings panel.

- **Shape**. Sets the direction to calculate the effector force.

    - **Point**. Point with omni-directional influence. Uses the object origin as the effector point.

    - **Line**. Field originates from the local z axis of the object.

    - **Plane**. Influences only in the local Z direction.

    - **Surface**. The force field acts on a 3D object's surface. In this case, the z axis is the surface normal.

    - **Every Point**. Uses every vertex in the mesh object as an effector point.

- **Strength**. The strength of the force field.

- **Flow**. Converts effector force into air flow velocity.

- **Domain Object**. Selects domain object of the smoke simulation.

- **Apply Density**. Adjust force strength based on smoke density.

The following are under the Falloff panel.

- **Shape**. Falloff type.

    - **Sphere**. The falloff is uniform in all directions.

    - **Tube**. The falloff results in a tube-shaped force field.

    - **Cone**. The falloff results in a cone-shaped force field.

- **Z Direction**. Effect in full or only positive/negative Z direction. There are three options for this one.

    - Both Z

    - Z+

    - Z-

- **Power**. How quickly strength falls off with distance from the force field.

- **Use minimum**. Use a minimum distance for the field's fall off.

- **Min Distance**. Minimum distance for the field's fall off.

- **Use maximum**. Use a maximum distance for the field to work.

Collision Physics

There are two different collision types that you may use: collision between different objects and internal collision. We should set one thing straight from the start: the primary targets of the collision calculation are the vertices of a soft body. So if you have too few vertices, too few collisions take place. Also, you can use edges and faces to improve the collision calculation.

Figure 5-98 shows its settings.

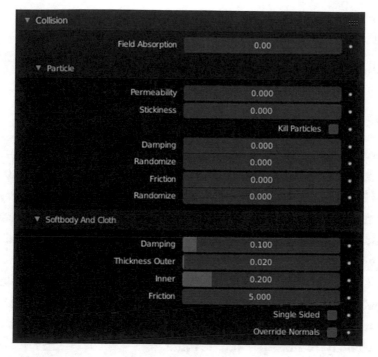

Figure 5-98. *Collision*

Let's briefly discuss the settings of this Physics type, which you can see in Figure 5-98.

- **Field Absorption**. The percentage of effector force that is lost during a collision with this object.

- **Particle ➤ Permeability**. Chance that the particle passes through the mesh.

- **Particle ➤ Stickiness**. The amount of stickiness to surface collision.

- **Particle ➤ Kill Particles**. Kill collided particles.

- **Particle ➤ Damping**. The amount of damping during particle collision.

- **Particle ➤ Randomize**. Random variation of damping.

- **Particle ➤ Friction**. The amount of friction during particle collision.

- **Particle ➤ Randomize**. Random variation of friction.

- **Softbody and Cloth ➤ Damping**. The amount of damping during softbody and cloth collision.

- **Softbody and Cloth ➤ Thickness Outer/Inner**. The amount of outer/inner thickness.

- **Softbody and Cloth ➤ Friction**. Friction of cloth collision.

Cloth Physics

Cloth simulation is one of the hardest aspects of CG, because it is a deceptively simple real-world item that is taken for granted, yet actually has very complex internal and environmental interactions. After years of development, Blender has a very robust cloth simulator that makes clothing, flags, banners, and so on. Cloth interacts with and is affected by other moving objects, the wind and other forces, and a general aerodynamic model—all of which is under your control.

A piece of cloth is any mesh, open or enclosed, that has been designated as cloth. The Cloth panels are located in the Physics tab and consist of three panels of options. Cloth is either an open or closed mesh and is mass-less, in that all cloth is assumed to have the same density, or mass per square unit.

Figure 5-99 shows the Cloth Physics settings.

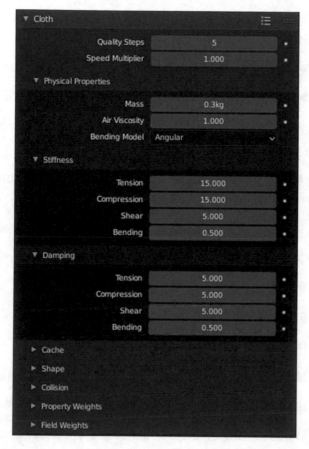

Figure 5-99. *Cloth*

If you have Blender 2.80 open, the Cache and Field Weights settings are the same as the ones discussed in Particles. Let's briefly discuss the other settings in this Physics type.

- **Quality Steps**. Quality of the simulation in steps per frame.

- **Speed Multiplier**. Cloth speed is multiplied by this value.

- **Physical Properties ➤ Mass**. Mass of cloth material.

- **Physical Properties ➤ Air Viscosity**. Air has normally thickness that slows falling things.

- **Physical Properties ➤ Bending Model**. Physical model for simulating bending forces. There are two types: Angular and Linear.

- **Stiffness ➤ Tension**. How much the material resists stretching. This is not present when Bending model is set to Linear.

- **Stiffness ➤ Compression**. How much the material resists compression.

- **Stiffness ➤ Shear**. How much the material resists shearing.

- **Stiffness ➤ Bending**. How much the material resists bending.

- **Damping ➤ Tension**. The amount of damping in stretching behavior. This is not present when Bending model is set to Linear.

- **Damping ➤ Compression**. The amount of damping in compression behavior.

- **Damping ➤ Shear**. The amount of damping in shearing behavior.

- **Damping ➤ Bending**. The amount of damping in bending behavior.

- **Shape ➤ Pin Group**. Vertex group for pinning of vertex.

- **Shape ➤ Stiffness**. Specifies the pin spring stiffness.

- **Shape ➤ Sewing**. Pulls loose edges together.

- **Shape ➤ Max Sewing Force**. Specifies the maximum sewing force.

- **Shape ➤ Shrinking Factor**. Factor by which to shrink cloth.

- **Shape ➤ Dynamic Mesh**. Make simulation respect deformations in the base mesh.

- **Collision ➤ Quality**. Specifies the number of collision iterations that should be done.

- **Object Collision ➤ Distance**. Specifies the minimum distance between collision objects before collision response takes effect.

- **Object Collision ➤ Impulse Clamping**. Specifies clamp collision impulses to avoid instability.

- **Object Collision ➤ Collision Collection**. Where you can limit colliders.

- **Self Collision ➤ Friction**. Specifies friction with self contact.

- **Self Collision ➤ Distance**. Minimum distance between cloth faces before collision response takes effect.

- **Self Collision ➤ Impulse Clamping**. Clamp collision impulses to avoid instability.

- **Self Collision ➤ Vertex Group**. Specifies the vertex group to define vertices that are not used during self collisions.

- **Property Weights ➤ Structural Group**. Vertex group for fine control over structural stiffness.

- **Property Weights ➤ Max Tension**. Specifies the maximum tension stiffness value.

- **Property Weights ➤ Max Compression**. Specifies the maximum compression stiffness value.

- **Property Weights ➤ Shear Group**. Vertex group for fine control over shear stiffness.

- **Property Weights ➤ Max Shearing**. Specifies the maximum shear scaling value.

- **Property Weights ➤ Bending Group**. Vertex group for fine control over bending stiffness.

- **Property Weights ➤ Max Bending**. Specifies the maximum bending value.

- **Property Weights ➤ Shrinking Group**. Vertex group for shrinking cloth.

- **Property Weights ➤ Max Shrinking**. Specifies the maximum amount to shrink by.

Dynamic Paint Physics

Dynamic Paint is a modifier and physics system that can turn objects into paint canvases and brushes, creating vertex colors, image sequences, or displacement. This makes many effects possible like, for example footsteps in the snow, raindrops that make the ground wet, paint that sticks to walls, or objects that gradually freeze.

Figure 5-100 shows its settings.

Figure 5-100. *Dynamic Paint*

The following settings appear after you click the **Add canvas** button.

- **Format**. Where you can choose a format for Dynamic paint. There are two options: Vertex and Image Sequence.

- **Anti-Aliasing**. Use 5x multi sampling to smooth paint edges.

- **Frame Start**. Indicates the staring frame.

- **Frame End**. Indicates the ending frame.

- **Frame Sub-steps**. Extra frames between scene frames to ensure smooth motion.

- **Subsurface Type**. Choose surface type. There are four options: Paint, Displace, Weight, and Waves.

- **Brush Collection**. Collections of brush objects.

- **Scale Influence**. Adjust influence brush objects have on this surface.

- **Radius**. Adjust radius of proximity brushes or particles for this surface.

Soft Body Physics

Soft Body simulates soft, deformable objects. It was designed primarily for adding secondary motion to animation, like jiggle for the body parts of a moving character.

The simulation works by combining existing animation on the object with forces acting on it. There are exterior forces like gravity or force fields and interior forces that hold the vertices together. This way you can simulate the shapes that an object would take on in reality if it had volume, was filled with something, and was acted on by real forces.

Figure 5-101 shows its settings.

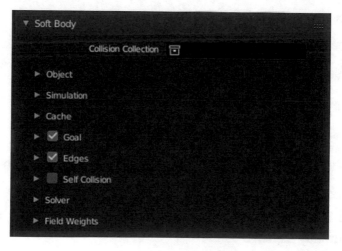

Figure 5-101. *Soft Body*

Let's briefly discuss the basic settings.

- **Object ➤ Friction**. Specifies the general media friction for point movements.

- **Object ➤ Mass**. Specifies the general mass value.

- **Object ➤ Control Point**. Specifies the control point mass values.

- **Simulation ➤ Speed**. Specifies the tweak timing for physics to control frequency and speed.

- **Goal ➤ Vertex Group**. Specifies the control point weight values.

- **Edges ➤ Springs**. Specifies the control point spring strength values.

- **Edges ➤ Pull**. Specifies the edge spring stiffness when longer than rest length.

- **Edges ➤ Push**. Specifies the edge spring stiffness when shorter than rest length.

- **Edges ➤ Length**. Specifies the alter spring length to shrink/blow up. 0 to disable.

- **Edges ➤ Collision Edge**. Edges collide too.

- **Edges ➤ Face**. Faces collide too.

- **Edges ➤ Damp**. Specifies the edge spring friction.

- **Edges ➤ Plastic**. Specifies the permanent deform.

- **Edges ➤ Blending**. Specifies the bending stiffness.

- **Self collision ➤ Calculation Type**. Where you can choose collision type.

- **Self Collision ➤ Ball Size**. Specifies the absolute ball size or factor if not manually adjusted.

- **Self Collision ➤ Stiffness**. Specifies the ball inflating pressure.

- **Self Collision ➤ Dampness**. Specifies the blending to inelastic collision.

- **Solver ➤ Step Size min/max**. Specifies the minimal/maximum number solver steps/frame.

- **Solver ➤ Auto-step**. Use velocities for automatic step sizes.

- **Solver ➤ Error Limit**. Specifies the Runge-Kutta ODE solver error limit; low values give more precision; high values give speed.

Fluid Physics

Fluid Physics simulate the physical properties of liquids especially water. While creating a scene in Blender, certain objects can be marked to participate in the fluid simulation. These can include but not limited to, being a fluid or as an obstacle. For a fluid simulation you have to have a domain to define the space that the simulation takes up. In the Domain settings, you can define the global simulation parameters (such as viscosity and gravity).

Fluid has seven types: Domain, Fluid, Obstacle, Inflow, Outflow, Control, and Particle. Let's briefly discuss the settings for each type.

Fluid ➤ Domain

Figure 5-102 shows the Domain settings.

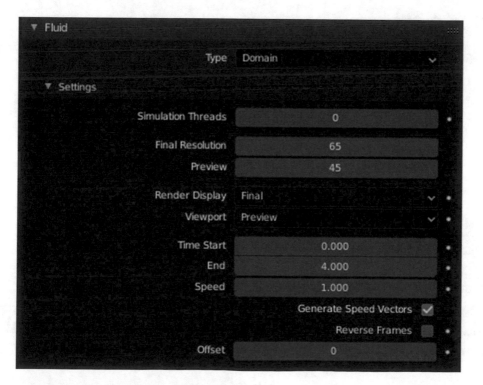

Figure 5-102. *Fluid Physics ➤ Domain Type*

- **Simulation Threads**. Override number of threads for the simulation.

- **Final Resolution**. Domain resolution in X, Y, and Z direction.

- **Preview**. Specifies the preview resolution in X, Y, and Z direction.

- **Render Display**. Where you can choose how to display the mesh for rendering.

- **Viewport**. Where you can choose how to display the mesh in the viewport.

- **Time Start/End**. Specifies the simulation time of the first/last blender frame in seconds.

- **Speed**. Specifies the fluid motion rate.

- **Generate Speed Vectors**. Generates speed vectors for vector blue.

- **Reverse Frames**. Reverses fluid frames.

- **Offset**. Specifies the offset when reading baked cache.

Fluid ➤ Outflow

Figure 5-103 shows the Outflow settings.

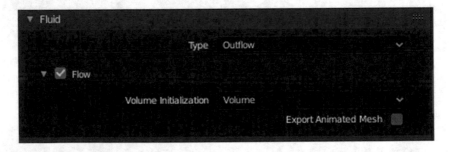

Figure 5-103. *Fluid Physics ➤ Outflow Type*

When you enable **Flow**, objects contribute to the fluid simulation. **Volume Initialization** is for common options among the different fluid types. There are three options. When you use **Volume**, the inside of the object is initialized as fluid all. This works only if the mesh is closed. When you use **Shell**, it is initialized as a thin fluid of the surface of the mesh. This can also be used if the mesh is open. **Both** can only be used in closed mesh and a mix of Volume and Shell. **Export Animated Mesh** exports the mesh as an animated one.

Fluid ➤ Control Type

Figure 5-104 shows the Control settings.

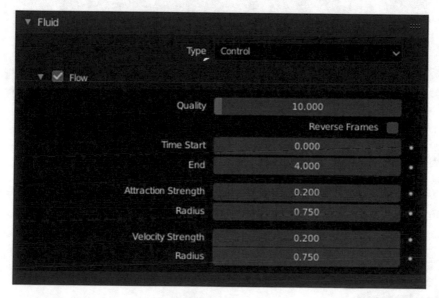

Figure 5-104. *Fluid Physics ➤ Control Type*

Quality is used for object sampling. **Reverse Frames** reverses the control of the object movement. **Time Start and End** specifies the time when the control particles are activated and deactivated. **Attraction Strength** specifies the force strength for directional attraction towards the control object. **Radius** specifies the force field radius around the control object. **Velocity Strength** specifies how much of the control object's velocity is influencing the fluid velocity. **Radius** specifies the force field radius around the control object.

Fluid ➤ Fluid

Figure 5-105 shows the Fluid settings.

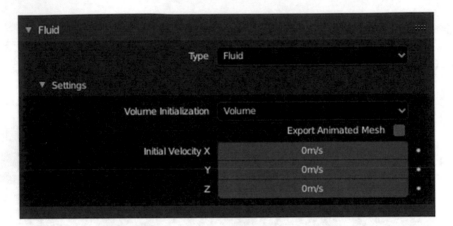

Figure 5-105. *Fluid Physics* ➤ *Fluid Type*

In Figure 5-105, Fluid type has settings similar to Outflow. These are Volume Initialization and Export Animated Mesh.

Initial Velocity is for the speed of the fluid at the beginning of the simulation (in meters per second).

Fluid ➤ Particle

Figure 5-106 shows the Particle settings.

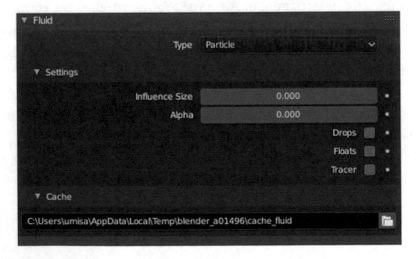

Figure 5-106. *Fluid Physics* ➤ *Particle Type*

Influence Size specifies the amount of particle size scaling. **Alpha** specifies the amount of particle alpha changes. With **Drops,** surface splashes of the fluid result in droplets being strewn about, like fresh water, with low Surface Tension. With **Floats,** the surface tension of fluid is higher and the fluid heavier, like cold seawater and soup. Breakaways are clumpier and fall back to the surface faster than Drops as with high Surface Tension. With **Tracer,** droplets follow the surface of the water where it existed, like a fog suspended above previous fluid levels.

Fluid Type ➤ Inflow

Figure 5-107 shows the Inflow settings.

Figure 5-107. *Fluid Physics ➤ Inflow Type*

In Figure 5-107, the Inflow settings are the same as Fluid Type. These are Volume Initialization, Exported Animated Mesh, and Initial Velocity, which is called **Inflow Velocity**.

When you enable **Local Coordinates**, it uses local coordinates for inflow.

Fluid Type ➤ Obstacle Type

Figure 5-108 shows the Obstacle settings.

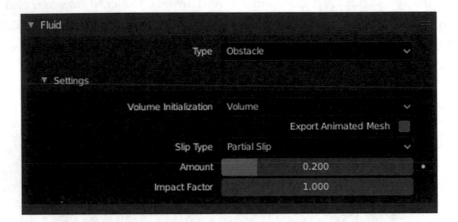

Figure 5-108. *Fluid Physics ➤ Obstacle Type*

The **Slip Type** setting is for the stickiness of the surface of the obstacle, to determine the tacky-surface. There are three options: Partial Slip (the default), No Slip, and Free Slip. **Amount** is where you specify the amount of mixing between no and free slip. 0 is no slip and 1 is free slip. **Impact Factor** is where you specify the value that controls the impact an obstacle has on the fluid. Making it zero behaves like outflow while greater than one results in high forces. One is the default.

Smoke Physics

Smoke simulation is a subset of the fluid system, can be used for simulating collections of airborne solids, liquid particulates, and gases, such as those that make up smoke. It simulates the fluid movement of air and generates animated voxel textures representing the density, heat, and velocity of other fluids or suspended particles that can be used for rendering.

Smoke Simulation have three types: Domain, Flow, and Collision. Each have their own settings.

Smoke ➤ Domain Type

Figure 5-109 shows the Domain settings.

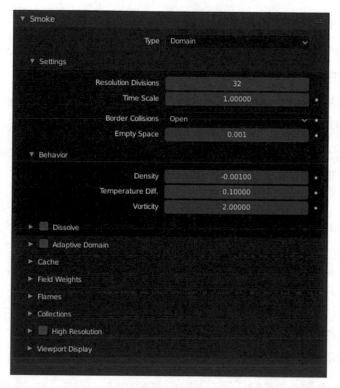

Figure 5-109.   *Smoke Simulation Physics ➤ Domain Type*

Let's discuss the basic settings of Domain Type.

- **Resolution Divisions**. Specifies the maximal resolution used in the fluid domain.

- **Time Scale**. Adjust simulation speed.

- **Border Collisions**. Where you select the domain border is treated as collision object.

- **Empty Space**. Value under which voxels are considered empty space to optimize caching and rendering.

- **Behavior ➤ Density**. How much density affects smoke motion.

- **Behavior ➤ Temperature Difference**. How much heat affects smoke motion.

- **Behavior ➤ Vorticity**. The amount of turbulence/rotation in fluid.

- **Dissolve ➤ Time**. Dissolving speed.

- **Adaptive Domain ➤ Add Resolution**. Maximum number of additional cells.

- **Adaptive Domain ➤ Margin**. Specifies the margin added around fluid to minimize boundary interference.

- **Adaptive Domain ➤ Threshold**. Specifies the maximum amount of fluid cell can contain before it is considered empty.

- **Flames ➤ Reaction Speed**. Specifies the speed of the burning reaction.

- **Flames ➤ Smoke**. Specifies the amount of smoke created by burning fuel.

- **Flames ➤ Vorticity**. Specifies the additional vorticity for the flames.

- **Flames ➤ Temperature Ignition**. Specifies the minimum temperature of flames.

- **Flames ➤ Maximum**. Specifies the maximum temperature of flames.

- **Flames ➤ Smoke Color**. Specifies the color of smoke emitted from burning fuel.

- **High resolution ➤ Resolution Divisions**. Enhance the resolution of smoke by this factor using noise.

- **High resolution ➤ Flow Sampling**. Where you can set method for sampling the high resolution flow. There are three options: Full sample, Linear and Nearest.

- **High resolution ➤ Noise Method**. Where you can set noise method, which creates the high resolution. There are two options: Wavelet and FFT.

- **High resolution ➤ Strength**. Specifies the strength of noise.

- **High resolution ➤ Show High Resolution**. Show high resolution using amplification.

Note   Vorticity is twice the angular velocity at a point in a fluid. Think of a small paddle wheel immersed in the fluid. If the fluid flow turns the paddle wheel, then it has velocity. Vorticity is a vector, and points out of the plane in which the fluids turns.

Smoke ➤ Collision Type

Figure 5-110 shows the Collision settings.

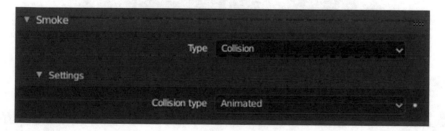

Figure 5-110. *Smoke Simulation Physics ➤ Collision Type*

Collision type of Smoke have a few settings. There are three types: Static, Rigid, and Animated.

Smoke ➤ Flow Type

Figure 5-111 shows the Flow settings.

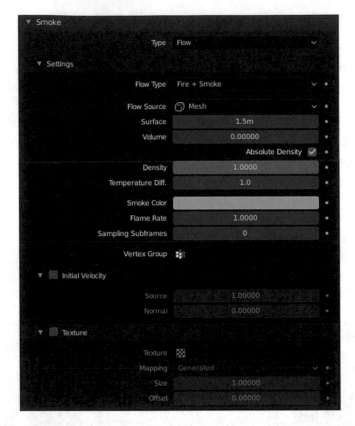

Figure 5-111. *Smoke Simulation Physics* ➤*Flow Type* ➤ *Fire +Smoke settings*

In the settings, there is Flow Type, where you can select the type of flow. There are four options: Smoke, Outflow, Fire+Smoke, and Fire. The settings varies by the option.

- **Flow Source** (Fire, Smoke, Fire+Smoke). Where you can change how smoke is emitted. There are two options: Mesh and Particle.

- **Surface** (Fire, Smoke, Fire+Smoke). Maximum distance from mesh surface to emit smoke.

- **Volume** (Fire, Smoke, Fire+Smoke). Factor for smoke emitted from inside the mesh volume.

- **Absolute Density** (Fire, Smoke, Fire+Smoke). Only allow given density value in temperature density.

- **Density** (Smoke, Fire+Smoke). Specifies the value for density.

- **Temperature Difference** (Smoke, Fire+Smoke). Specifies the temperature difference to ambient temperature.

- **Smoke Color** (Smoke, Fire+Smoke). Specifies the color of smoke.

- **Flame Rate** (Fire, Fire+Smoke). Specifies the flame rate.

- **Sampling Subframes** (Fire, Smoke, Fire+Smoke). Number of additional samples to take between frames to improve quality of fast moving flows.

- **Vertex Group** (Fire, Outflow, Smoke, Fire+Smoke). The name of the vertex group that determines the surface emission rate.

- **Initial Velocity ➤ Source** (Fire, Smoke, Fire+Smoke). Multiplier of source velocity passed to smoke.

- **Initial Velocity ➤ Normal** (Fire, Smoke, Fire+Smoke). The amount of normal directional velocity.

- **Texture ➤ Texture** (Fire, Outflow, Smoke, Fire+Smoke). Specifies texture that controls emission strength.

- **Texture ➤ Mapping** (Fire, Outflow, Smoke, Fire+Smoke). Where you can choose texture mapping. There are two options: Generated and UV.

- **Texture ➤ Size** (Fire, Outflow, Smoke, Fire+Smoke). Specifies the size of texture mapping.

- **Texture ➤ Offset** (Fire, Outflow, Smoke, Fire+Smoke). Specifies the Z-offset of texture mapping.

Rigid Body Physics

Figure 5-112 shows the Rigid Body settings.

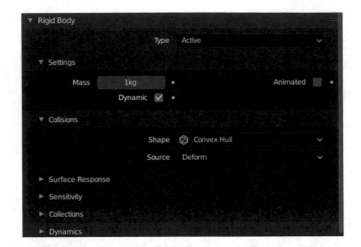

Figure 5-112. *Rigid Body physics*

The Rigid Body simulation simulates the motion of solid objects. It affects the position and orientation of objects and does not deform them.

Unlike the other simulations in Blender, the rigid body simulation works closer with the animation system. This means that rigid bodies can be used like regular objects and be part of parent-child relationships, animation constraints, and drivers.

So, let's briefly discuss its settings.

- **Type**. Role of object in Rigid Body Simulation. There are two types: Passive and Active.

- **Mass**. Specifies how much the object weighs, irrespective of gravity. Only present in Active Type.

- **Dynamic**. Rigid body actively participate to the simulation. Only present in Active type.

- **Animated**. Allows Rigid Body to be controlled by the animation system.

- **Collisions ➤ Shape**. Choose the collision shape of object in Rigid Body Simulation. There are seven options: Box, Sphere, Capsule, Cylinder, Cone, Convex Hull, and Mesh. By default, it is set to Convex Hull.

- **Collision Source ➤ Source**. Set the source of mesh to create collision shape. This setting is only present when Shape is set to Convex Hull or Mesh.

- **Surface Response ➤ Friction**. Resistance of object to movement.

- **Surface Response ➤ Bounciness**. Tendency of object to bounce after colliding with another.

- **Sensitivity ➤ Collision Margin**. Uses custom collision margin. This setting is not present when the Shape setting under Collision is set to Cone Shape.

- **Sensitivity ➤ Margin**. Threshold of distance near surface where collisions are still considered.

- **Collections**. Collision collections rigid body belongs to.

Rigid Body Constraints (Physics)

Constraints, also known as joints, for rigid bodies connect two rigid bodies. Figure 5-113 shows its settings.

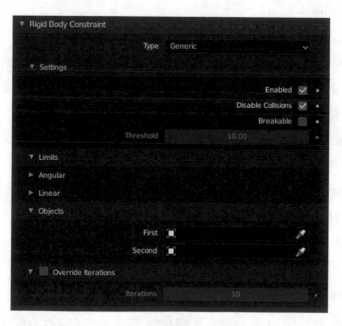

Figure 5-113. *Rigid Body Constraints Physics*

The physics constraints are meant to be attached to an Empty object. The constraint has fields that can be pointed at the two physics-enabled object that is bound by the constraint. The Empty object provides a location and axis for the constraint distinct from the two constrained objects. The location of the entity hosting the physics constraint marks a location and set of axes on each of the two constrained objects. These two anchor points are calculated at the beginning of the animation and their position and orientation remain fixed in the local coordinate system of the object for the duration of the animation. The objects can move far from the constraint object, but the constraint anchor moves with the object. If this feature seems limiting, consider using multiple objects with a non-physics child of constraint and animate the relative location of the child.

- **Type**. Sets the type of rigid body constraint. There are eight types: Fixed, Point, Hinge, Slider, Piston, Generic, Generic Spring, and Motor. Fixed is the default type set in this setting.

- **Enabled**. Enables the constraint.

- **Disable Collision**. Disables collisions between constrained rigid bodies.

- **Breakable**. Constraint can be broken if it receives an impulse above the threshold.

- **Threshold**. Impulse threshold that must be reached for the constraint to break.

- **Angular ➤ X angle**. Limits the rotation around the x axis. Only active when type is set to Generic.

- **Angular ➤ X Lower/Upper**. Specifies the lower/upper limit of the x-axis rotation. Only active when type is set to Generic.

- **Angular ➤ Y angle**. Limits the rotation around the y axis. Only active when type is set to Generic.

- **Angular ➤ Y Lower/Upper**. Specifies the lower/upper limit of the y-axis rotation. Only active when type is set to Generic.

- **Angular ➤ Z angle**. Limits the rotation around the z axis.

- **Angular ➤ Z Lower/Upper**. Specifies the lower/upper limit of the z-axis rotation. Only active when type is set to Hinge, Piston or Generic.

- **Angular ➤ Target Velocity**. Specifies target angular motor velocity. Only active when type is set to motor.

- **Angular ➤ Max Impulse**. Specifies maximum angular motor impulse. Only active when type is set to motor.

- **Linear ➤ X Axis**. Limit translation on the x axis. Only active when Type is set to Piston and Generic.

- **Linear ➤ X Lower/Upper**. Specifies the lower/upper limit of the x-axis translation. Only active when Type is set to Piston and Generic.

- **Linear ➤ Y Axis**. Limit translation on the y axis. Only active when Type is set to Generic.

- **Linear ➤ Y Lower/Upper**. Specifies the lower/upper limit of the y-axis translation. Only active when Type is set to Generic.

- **Linear ➤ Z Axis**. Limit translation on the z axis. Only active when Type is set to Generic.

- **Linear ➤ Z Lower/Upper**. Specifies Lower/Upper limit of the z-axis translation. Only active when Type is set to Generic.

- **Linear ➤ Target Velocity**. Specifies target linear motor velocity. Only active when type is set to motor.

- **Linear ➤ Max Impulse**. Specifies maximum linear motor impulse. Only active when type is set to motor.

- **Objects ➤ First/Second**. Specifies First/Second Rigid Body to be constrained.

- **Override ➤ Iterations**. Specifies number of constraint solver iterations needs per simulation step.

To learn more about how to use Blender Physics, visit `https://docs.blender.org/manual/en/latest/physics/index.html`.

I'd like for you to read Blender Manual since most of the information came from it. For now, it isn't fully updated. You can also learn a lot from Blender Stack Exchange and Blenderartist.org, where I also got some of the information. Communicating with other 3D artists and researching are also essential.

CHAPTER 6

The Future of Game Engines

In this chapter, I'll talk about the Blender game engine. It was announced that the game engine is not included in version 2.80. If that's so, is there an open source alternative that is the same as or better? Is there a possibility that we will see the Blender game engine in future releases?

Let's start the discussion.

The Blender Game Engine

The Blender game engine has been used by many 3D artists and developers since 2000. This engine uses a system of graphical *logic bricks* to control the movement and display of objects. The game engine can also be extended via a set of Python bindings.

The Blender game engine is Blender's tool for real-time projects, from architectural visualization and simulations to games. It allows you to create interactive 3D applications or simulations. The major difference between the game engine and the conversational Blender system is in the rendering process. In a normal Blender engine, images and animations are built offline; once rendered, they cannot be modified. Conversely, the Blender game engine renders scenes continuously in real time and incorporates facilities for user interaction during the rendering process.

The Blender game engine also oversees a game loop, which processes logic, sound, physics, and rendering simulations in sequential order. The engine is written in C++. The user has access to a powerful, high-level, event-driven logic editor that is comprised of a series of specialized components called *logic bricks*. The logic editor provides deep interaction with the simulation, and its functionality can be extended through Python scripting. It is designed to abstract the complex engine features into a simple user interface, which does not require programming experience.

© Ezra Thess Mendoza Guevarra 2020

E. T. M. Guevarra, *Modeling and Animation Using Blender*, https://doi.org/10.1007/978-1-4842-5340-3_6

There are several powerful libraries that the game engine uses.

- **Audaspace**: A sound library for control audio.

- **Bullet**: A physics engine featuring 3D collision detection, soft-body dynamics, and rigid-body dynamics.

- **Detour**: A pathfinding and spatial reasoning toolkit.

- **Recast**: A state-of-the-art navigation mesh construction toolset of games.

Figure 6-1 shows the version 2.79b Blender game engine.

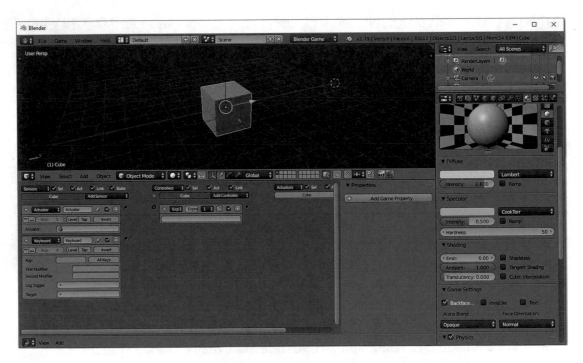

Figure 6-1. *Blender game engine 2.79B*

You already know how the Blender game engine works. You might feel that it is really a powerful tool, and you are asking why the team stopped developing this engine. In Figure 6-1, the tools are in the current version. Well, for anyone who is talented, it doesn't matter if your tools are from the Jurassic era or from the future. I personally think that the team is trying to make Blender easier to learn.

So, what do we have for now?

UPBGE

When I researched about the Blender game engine's future, this render engine name came up: UPBGE, or Uchronia Project Blender game engine. It is an open source 3D game engine formed from the old Blender game engine and deployed with Blender itself. This unified workflow is its main strength, as you can make your game from start to finish with UPBGE.

It features real-time advanced physics powered by Bullet, including rigid bodies, soft bodies, obstacles simulation, and pathfinding. It has a fully integrated audio engine powered by OpenAL and SDL, supports 3D sound and sound effects, and provides an easy and straightforward visual logic system.

It also has advanced features, such as PBR materials and powerful Python language bindings and components that allow support to even more libraries through the use of PyPI, Render attachments, fake or real-time reflections settings directly through the interface, and an HDR pipeline.

Figure 6-2 shows the UPBGE user interface.

Figure 6-2. *UPBGE 2.4 user interface*

You can download UPBGE from `https://upbge.org/index.html`.

Armory3D

Armory3D is another 3D game engine that I came across. It is an open source software 3D game engine with full Blender integration, which turns it into a complete game development tool. It offers a unified workflow from start to finish, making your work faster. No more jumping between different applications to constantly export data.

Behind the scenes, Armory3D is powered by open source technology. Utilizing Kha, a multimedia framework, and Haxe, a cross-platform toolkit, it provides first-class performance and portability.

Armory3D is based on the Cycles nodes. Materials are precompiled into shaders suitable for real-time rendering. Every scene in Armory3D is renderable as-is in Cycles using pathtracing. This makes it possible to use Cycles for light baking with no separate setup. Everything is bundled to provide the ultimate game development tool. As a starting point, you can choose one of the available game prototype templates. The code editor has integrated debugging support. You can use nodes, write scripts in Haxe, or embed WebAssembly code. You can also create live scenes and export them to desktop, web, and mobile consoles, so everyone can experience them. A binary data format, asset compression, and efficient build tools are developed to prevent bloated package sizes. A robust animation system is employed, with support for GPU skinning, action blending, and events. On top of that, each node can be animated in a timeline using keyframes, just like you are used to.

Figure 6-3 is a sneak peek at the Armory3D user interface.

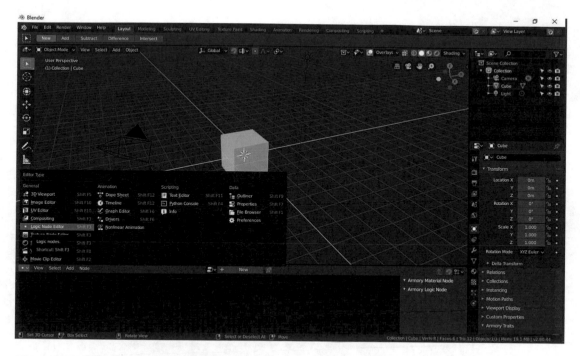

Figure 6-3. *Armory 06 3D user interface*

You can download Armory3D from https://armory3d.org.

In Figure 6-3, UPBGE is using the Blender 2.7x version User Interface. UPBGE is currently developing their version for Blender 2.80, while Armory3D is already using version 2.80. But this is the key; these engines are using their own version of Blender while improving the logic node editor in it. Blender 2.80 doesn't have a logic editor but the Armory3D team included it to give us a game engine on par with other game engines in the market. UPBGE is also developing its current logic editor to give us a game engine that will make things easy for us based on Blender's current version. This is the power of a GNU GPL license.

I have talked about open source 3D game engines, but is there any future for the Blender game engine?

The Future of the Blender Game Engine

There are a lot of questions on the Internet about the future of the Blender game engine. Ton Roosendaal answers this question. Figure 6-4 shows his Twitter post regarding this topic.

Figure 6-4. *Ton Roosendaal's answer on Twitter*

Based on this answer, based on the development of current Blender 2.80 builds, we can assume that the Blender game engine (at least for now) is at rest. Epic games and Unreal made a huge donation, so we can hope that they might also develop Blender to have a better game engine. If it returns to the spotlight, it is up to the Blender team. For now, we can enjoy Eevee and the open source game engines available there. Creativity is not bound by the tools that we have.

APPENDIX A

Index of Refraction

Some Representative Refractive Indices

Vacuum	1.000
Air at STP	1.000277

Gases at 0°C (Celsius) and 1 atm

Air	1.000293
Carbon dioxide	1.001
Helium	1.000036
Hydrogen	1.000132

Liquids at 20°C

Arsenic trisulfide/sulfur in methylene iodide	1.9
Carbon disulfide	1.628
Benzene	1.501
Carbon tetrachloride	1.461
Silicone oil	1.393–1.403
Kerosene	1.39
Ethanol (ethyl alcohol)	1.361
Acetone	1.36
Water	1.330

(*continued*)

© Ezra Thess Mendoza Guevarra 2020
E. T. M. Guevarra, *Modeling and Animation Using Blender*, https://doi.org/10.1007/978-1-4842-5340-3

10% glucose solution in water	1.3477
20% glucose solution in water	1.3635
60% glucose solution in water	1.4394

Solids at Room Temperature

Gold	0.470
Bronze	1.180
Silicon carbide (Moissanite; 6H form)	2.65
Titanium dioxide (Rutile phase)	2.614
Diamond	2.417
Strontium titanate	2.41
Tantalum pentoxide	2.15
Amber	1.55
Sodium chloride	1.544
Fused silica (a pure form of glass)	1.458
Copper	1.100–2.430

Other Materials

Liquid helium	1.025
Water/ice	1.31
Teflon AF	1.315
Cryolite	1.338
Cytop	1.34
Teflon	1.35–1.38
25 % sugar solution	1.3723
Human cornea	1.373/1.380/1.401
Human lens	1.386–1.406
Human liver	1.369
Human intestine	1.329–1.338

Aluminum	1.390–1.440
Acrylic glass	1.490–1.492
50% sugar solution	1.4200
Polylactic acid	1.46
Pyrex (a borosilicate glass)	1.470
Vegetable oil	1.47
Glycerol	1.4729
75% sugar solution	1.4774
PMMA	1.4893–1.4899
Rock salt	1.516
Window glass (plate glass)	1.52
Crown glass (pure)	1.50–1.54
PETg	1.57
Asphalt	1.635
Polycarbonate	1.60
Emerald	1.560–1.605
Crown glass (impure)	1.485–1.755
Flint glass (pure)	1.60–1.62
Bromine	1.661
Pearl	1.530–1690
Flint glass (impure)	1.523–1.925
Sapphire	1.762–1.778
Crystal	2.000
Cubic zirconia	2.15–2.18
Potassium niobate	2.28
Zinc oxide	2.4
Mercury sulfide	3.02
Silicon	3.42–3.48

APPENDIX B

HotKeys

General	
New	Ctrl+N
Open	Ctrl+O
Open Recent	Shift+Ctrl+O
Save	Ctrl+S
Save As	Shift+Ctrl+S
Quit	Ctrl+Q
Undo	Ctrl+Z
Redo	Shift+Ctrl+Z
Add mesh/Add nodes	Shift+A
Operator Search	F3
Render Image	F12
View Render	F11
Play Animation	spacebar
Render Animation	Ctrl+F12
View Animation	Ctrl+F11
Opening Toolbar	T
Opening Sidebar	N
Quick Favorites	Q
Mode Type Pie Menu	Ctrl+Tab
Shading Type Pie Menu	Z

(continued)

© Ezra Thess Mendoza Guevarra 2020

E. T. M. Guevarra, *Modeling and Animation Using Blender*, https://doi.org/10.1007/978-1-4842-5340-3

Move Objects to Collection	M
Create New Collection	Ctrl+G
Select All	A
Undo Selection	Alt+A
Invert Selection	Ctrl+I
Circle Selection	C
Join Objects	Ctrl+J
Insert Animation Keyframes	I
Delete Animation Keyframes	Alt+I
Delete Objects	X
Hide Selected Objects	H
Show Hidden Objects	Alt+H

Views/Navigation

Perspective/Orthographic	Numpad+5
Camera	Numpad+0
Top	Numpad+7
Bottom	Ctrl+Numpad+7
Front	Numpad+1
Back	Ctrl+Numpad+1
Right	Numpad+3
Left	Ctrl+Numpad+3
Orbit Left	Numpad+4
Orbit Right	Numpad+6
Orbit Up	Numpad+8
Orbit Down	Numpad+2
Orbit Opposite	Numpad+9
Pan Left	Ctrl+Numpad+4

Pan Right	Ctrl+Numpad+6
Pan Up	Ctrl+Numpad+8
Pan Down	Ctrl+Numpad+2
Roll Left	Shift+Numpad+4+
Roll Right	Shift+Numpad+6
Zoom In	Numpad++
Zoom Out	Numpad+-
Zoom Region	Shift+B
Render Region	Ctrl+B
Clear render Region	Ctrl+Alt+B
Toggle Quad View	Ctrl+Alt+Q
Toggle Maximize Area	Ctrl+spacebar
Toggle Fullscreen Area	Ctrl+Alt+spacebar

Switching Editors

File Browser	Shift+F1
Movie Clip	Shift+F2
Shade Editor	Shift+F3
Python Console	Shift+F4
3D View	Shift+F5
Graph Editor	Shift+F6
Properties	Shift+F7
Video Sequencer	Shift+F8
Outliner	Shift+F9
Image Editor	Shift+F10
Text Editor	Shift+F11
Dope Sheet	Shift+F12

(*continued*)

Tools per Workspace/Editor/Modes
(Hotkey in Toolbar: spacebar+< tool hotkey >)
(To access the Annotate tools by their own hotkeys, u
se Shift+D+spacebar at first access)

Layout Workspace

Select	W
Select Box	B
Select Circle	C
Select Lasso	L
Cursor	spacebar
Move	G
Rotate	R
Scale	S
Scale Cage	3
Transform	T
Annotate	5+or+D
Annotate Line	6+or+D
Annotate Polygon	7+or+D
Annotate Eraser	8+or+D
Measure	M

Modeling Workspace and Edit Mode
(Select to Annotate Eraser tool is the same as in Layout Workspace)

Extrude Region	E
Extrude Along Normals	9
Extrude Individuals	0
Extrude to Cursor	Shift+1
Inset Faces	I

Bevel	Ctrl+B
Loop Cut	Ctrl+R
Offset Edge Loop Cut	Shift+Ctrl+R
Knife	K
Bisect	Shift+2
Polybuild	Shift+3
Spin	Shift+4
Spin Duplicate	Shift+5
Smooth	Shift+6
Randomize	Shift+7
Edge Slide	Shift+8
Vertex Slide	Shift+V
Shrink/Flatten	Alt+S
Push/Pull	Shift+9
Shear	Shift+Ctrl+Alt+S
To Sphere	Shift+Alt+S
Rip Region	V
Rip Edge	Alt+D

Sculpting Workspace and Sculpt mode

Draw	X
Clay	C
Clay Stripes	1
Layer	L
Inflate	I
Blob	2
Crease	Shift+C
Smooth	S

(continued)

Flatten	Shift+T
Fill	3
Scrape	4
Pinch	P
Grab	G
Snake Hook	K
Thumb	5
Nudge	6
Rotate	7
Simplify	8
Mask	9
Box Mask	B
Lasso Mask	0
Box Hide	Shift+H
Annotate	Shift+1
Annotate Line	Shift+2
Annotate Polygon	Shift+3
Annotate Eraser	Shift+4

UV Editing Workspace (UV Editor)
(Select to Transform tool is the same as in Layout Workspace)

Annotate	4
Annotate Line	5
Annotate Polygon	6
Annotate Eraser	7
Grab	
Relax	9
Pinch	0

Texture Paint Workspace (Image Editor in Paint Mode)

Draw (*same as Texture Paint mode*)	1
Soften (*same as Texture Paint mode*)	2
Smear (*same as Texture Paint mode*)	3
Clone (*same as Texture Paint mode*)	4
Fill (*same as Texture Paint mode*)	5
Mask (*same as Texture Paint mode*)	6
Annotate (*only in Texture Paint mode*)	7
Annotate Line (*only in Texture Paint mode*)	8
Annotate Polygon (*only in Texture Paint mode*)	9
Annotate Eraser (*only in Texture Paint mode*)	0

Layout Workspace in Weight Paint and Vertex Paint

Draw (Weight Paint and Vertex Paint)	1
Blur (Weight Paint and Vertex Paint)	2
Average (Weight Paint and Vertex Paint)	3
Smear (Weight Paint and Vertex Paint)	4
Gradient (Weight Paint Only)	5
Sample Weight (Weight Paint Only)	6
Sample Vertex Group (Weight Paint Only)	7
Annotate	5+(Weight)+8+(Vertex)
Annotate Line	6+(Weight)+9+(Vertex)
Annotate Polygon	7+(Weight)+0+(Vertex)
Annotate Eraser	8+(Weight)+Shift+1+(Vertex)

Index

© Ezra Thess Mendoza Guevarra 2020
E. T. M. Guevarra, *Modeling and Animation Using Blender*, https://doi.org/10.1007/978-1-4842-5340-3

Printed in the United States
By Bookmasters